Praise for *Key Management Development Models*

An accessible and interesting book – a great resource for all those looking to develop and hone their skills as managers.

LUCY DALY, PROGRAMME DIRECTOR, MANCHESTER BUSINESS SCHOOL

A very practical, engaging guide to the essential tools which managers at all levels need to be effective themselves and to develop others. Highly recommended.

STUART CHAMBERS, FORMER CEO OF PILKINGTON PLC

I found Cotton's book very helpful. It is clearly written and superbly set out. I recommend it to any budding and established manager.

PROFESSOR DENNIS KAVANAGH, UNIVERSITY OF LIVERPOOL

David Cotton has compiled a short compendium of accepted behavioural theory. As such, it provides an excellent reference point for those seeking to understand how to achieve improvement in themselves and others. Its application is business but the concepts are universal.

RICHARD C. BAILEY, ROTHSCHILD PARTNER, NON EXECUTIVE DIRECTOR, BUSINESS MANAGER

Key Management Development Models

DAVID COTTON

Key Management Development Models

70+ tools for developing yourself and managing others

PEARSON

Harlow, England • London • New York • Boston • San Francisco • Toronto • Sydney
Auckland • Singapore • Hong Kong • Tokyo • Seoul • Taipei • New Delhi
Cape Town • São Paulo • Mexico City • Madrid • Amsterdam • Munich • Paris • Milan

Pearson Education Limited
Edinburgh Gate
Harlow CM20 2JE
United Kingdom
Tel: +44 (0)1279 623623
Web: www.pearson.com/uk

First published 2015 (print and electronic)

ISBN: 978-1-292-09322-2 (print)
        978-1-292-11052-3 (PDF)
        978-1-292-11053-0 (ePub)
        978-1-292-11051-6 (eText)

British Library Cataloguing-in-Publication Data
A catalogue record for the print edition is available from the British Library

Library of Congress Cataloging-in-Publication Data
Cotton, David, 1955- author.
  Key management development models : 70+ tools for developing yourself and managing others / David Cotton.
    pages cm
  Includes index.
  ISBN 978-1-292-09322-2
  1. Executive ability. 2. Management. 3. Supervision. I. Title.
HD38.2.C665 2015
658.4'07124—dc23
                                            2015025852

Print edition typeset in 9.25 Helvetica Neue Pro by 71
Print edition printed by Ashford Colour Press Ltd, Gosport

NOTE THAT ANY PAGE CROSS REFERENCES REFER TO THE PRINT EDITION

Contents

About the author xi
Acknowledgements xii
Preface xiii
Using this book xv

DEVELOPING YOURSELF

PART ONE Happiness 2

1 Positive affirmations 4
2 Positive mental attitude and content reframing 6

PART TWO Memory and recall 8

3 Loci method 10
4 Number/rhyme method 12

PART THREE Motivation 14

5 Maslow's hierarchy of needs 16
6 Glasser's choice theory 18
7 Pink's model of motivation 21

PART FOUR Personal change 23

8 Cognitive restructuring 25
9 *The Secret*/law of attraction (Byrne) 28
10 Seven habits of highly effective people (Covey) 30

PART FIVE Problem solving and decision making 33

11 Force field analysis 35
12 Is/is not problem-solving technique 38
13 Ladder of inference (Argyris) 41
14 OODA loop 44
15 Polarity management 46
16 Vroom–Yetton–Jago decision model 49

PART SIX Resilience 52

17 | Kobasa and 'hardiness' 54

PART SEVEN Self-awareness 56

18 | 360° feedback 58
19 | Emotional intelligence 60
20 | Johari window 63
21 | Multiple intelligences 66

PART EIGHT Self-confidence and stress management 69

22 | Anchoring a calm state 71
23 | Meditation 73
24 | Mindfulness 75

PART NINE Time management, concentration and focus 78

25 | Covey's time matrix (Eisenhower) 80
26 | Getting things done (Allen) 83
27 | Wheel of life 85

PART TEN Learning 88

28 | Accelerated learning 90
29 | Benziger's thinking styles assessment 93
30 | Kolb/Honey and Mumford learning styles 96

PART ELEVEN Listening skills 100

31 | Active listening 102
32 | Critical listening 105
33 | Relationship listening 107

MANAGING OTHERS

PART TWELVE Assertiveness 110

34 | The broken record 112
35 | Fogging 114

PART THIRTEEN Coaching 116

36 CLEAR model (Hawkins) 118
37 GROW model (Whitmore *et al.*) 120
38 Solution-focused coaching (OSKAR) 123

PART FOURTEEN Communication 126

39 DISC 128
40 Matching and mirroring 134
41 Storytelling 136
42 VAK (visual, auditory, kinaesthetic) 143

PART FIFTEEN Conflict management 147

43 Betari box 149
44 Thomas–Kilmann conflict mode instrument 151

PART SIXTEEN Creativity 154

45 Brain-friendly brainstorming 156
46 Challenging assumptions 159
47 PMI (plus, minus, interesting) 161
48 Random word technique 163
49 SCAMPER 166

PART SEVENTEEN Giving feedback 168

50 EEC model 170
51 EENC 172

PART EIGHTEEN Goal setting 175

52 Locke and Latham's five principles 177
53 Reticular activating system 179
54 SMART goals 181
55 CASE – behavioural objectives 184

PART NINETEEN Influence and persuasion 186

56 | 4Ps of persuasion 188
57 | Bilateral brain theory 191
58 | Embedded commands 194
59 | Locus of control (Weiner's attribution theory) 197
60 | Positive language 200
61 | Spheres of influence 202

PART TWENTY Leadership 205

62 | Action-centred leadership 207
63 | Covert leadership 210
64 | Leadership styles 213

PART TWENTY-ONE Negotiation 219

65 | Distributive bargaining (adversarial model) 221
66 | Integrative bargaining 223
67 | Harvard principled negotiation 226
68 | RADPAC 229

PART TWENTY-TWO Presentation 232

69 | INTRO 234

PART TWENTY-THREE Relationships 237

70 | The four agreements (Ruiz) 239
71 | Rapport building 243
72 | Transactional analysis 245

PART TWENTY-FOUR Teamwork 249

73 | Sigmoid curve 251
74 | Tick-box and high-performance teams 255
75 | Extended Tuckman teamwork theory 259

Index 263

About the author

David Cotton spent 21 years with Arthur Andersen and PwC before becoming a freelance trainer in 2002. He has worked on 4 continents and in 40 countries, delivering a wide range of training in management, leadership, communication skills, business networking, confidence building, dealing with difficult people, change management, business strategy, coaching and mentoring.

His clients span local and national government and nearly every industry sector, and include the European Parliament, European Commission and many of its agencies, the United Nations, BBC, Syrian Ministry for Foreign Affairs, Russian Federal Commission, Croatian MoD, PwC, most of the major Middle Eastern oil and gas companies, Manchester Business School and many others.

David has published a dozen books and scores of journal articles.

Acknowledgements

Thank you very much to Jane, Philippa and Victoria Cotton for love and support; Clair Taylor for wise counsel; Liz and Harry Cotton for bringing yin and yang to life; and David Crosby and the editorial team at Pearson.

Publisher's acknowledgements

We are grateful to the following for permission to reproduce copyright material:

Figures
Figure 13.1 adapted from *Overcoming Organizational Defenses: Facilitating organizational learning* (1st ed.), Pearson Education, Inc. (Argyris, C. 1990), p. 88, Figure 5.1, Copyright © 1990, reprinted and electronically reproduced by permission of Pearson Education, Inc., New York; Figures 15.1 and 15.2 after *Polarity Management: Identifying and managing unsolvable problems,* HRD Press (Johnson, B. 1996), Copyright © 1992, 1996, reprinted by permission of the publisher, HRD Press, Amherst, MA, (800) 822-2801, www.hrdpress.com; Figure 19.1 after Daniel Goleman, 'An EI-based theory of performance' in *The Emotionally Intelligent Workplace: How to select for, measure, and improve emotional intelligence in individuals, groups, and organizations,* p. 28, Figure 3.1 (Cherniss, C. and Goleman, D. (eds.) 2001), Copyright © 2001 by Cary Cherniss and Daniel Goleman, reproduced with permission of John Wiley & Sons; Figure 25.1 adapted from *The 7 Habits of Highly Effective People*, Simon & Schuster (Covey, S.R. 2004), p. 151, ISBN 978-0684858395, copied with permission of Franklin Covey Co.; Figure 27.1 based on Paul J. Meyer's Wheel of Life, © Success Motivation International, www.success-motivation.com; Figures 30.1 and 30.2 adapted from *Experiential Learning: Experience as the source of learning and development*, Prentice Hall, Inc. (Kolb, D.A. 1983), p. 42, Copyright © 1983, reprinted and electronically reproduced by permission of Pearson Education, Inc., New York; Figure 30.3 after *The Manual of Learning Styles,* 3rd revised ed., Peter Honey Publications (Honey, P. and Mumford, A. 1992).

In some instances we have been unable to trace the owners of copyright material, and we would appreciate any information that would enable us to do so.

Preface

The statistician George Box* (1919–2013) wrote that 'essentially, all models are wrong, but some are useful'. Models are wrong in that they are, inevitably, generalisations and for every generalised statement you can find exceptions. They are useful in that they help us to make sense of the world.

A well-constructed business model distils knowledge and information into an easily understood framework which can be applied in new situations. The best models are timeless and those represented in this book range from 3,000 years ago to the modern day.

This book aims to capture some of the best models, some old, some new, which will help you in two areas: to develop your skills as a manager and to develop those who report to you. Inevitably, there is overlap between the two sections; if a model helps you to develop yourself, you can use it in coaching and mentoring others and you can apply a model which is designed to develop others to develop yourself. In this sense, there is a slightly artificial division between the two parts of the book.

Whether or not you have direct reports at work, many of the models will help you to improve your working relationships in every direction. The book is designed for anyone who wants to develop their professional skills and credibility and anyone who wants to improve their management ability or their working relationships. There is as much here for the business leader as for the business newcomer, for the new manager and for the experienced manager alike.

I selected some models because of their simplicity. They are easy to understand and apply and their real power comes from that very simplicity. Other models are designed to help you to reflect on your current management practice and see it from new perspectives.

Several things became apparent as I was selecting the models:

- There is little new under the sun. Some of the ideas captured in relatively new models echo sentiments expressed in books that are centuries old.

- The big ideas found in new models are often hybrids of other ideas.

- At the heart of many of the models is a desire to communicate better and be better understood.

- The best tools are relatively simple to understand but it can take considerable practice to apply them effortlessly.

*Box, G.E.P. and Draper, N.R. (1987) *Empirical Model-Building and Response Surfaces.* New York: John Wiley & Sons, p. 424.

In time you will start to see relationships between the models. Some concur, some complement and some conflict with each other, but each offers a perspective on how we think, act, learn or behave and opens windows on how to improve our performance in each area.

Imagine that you need help in motivating your team members. Abraham Maslow will tell you that needs are hierarchical, so that as we meet a particular need, we move to another level of need. His student William Glasser will argue that needs are not hierarchical but work independently of each other. It matters little who is correct; what matters is that the models give you sufficient food for thought to begin to see what will motivate the individuals who report to you.

The best models give us 'Aha!' moments – because they crystallise our thoughts, expand our horizons, confirm our existing thinking or add structure to something which had hitherto seemed vague or abstract. They offer steps to follow, a fresh approach or a new insight.

I hope that you find the ideas here of great personal and professional value.

David Cotton

Using this book

Key Management Development Models describes more than 70 models and frameworks which will help you to develop yourself to become a more effective manager and to develop others to perform at a higher level. While you could read it from beginning to end as a fairly comprehensive collection of tools to enhance your management ability, it may be better to:

- skim through the book the first time, picking out models and ideas that jump out at you, either because they look interesting or because they are directly applicable to your current situation, then

- use the contents pages to focus on a particular area of need, skim through the models in the appropriate section, then read in more detail the one that best fits your situation.

The models are divided into two main sections:

1 **Developing yourself**: these models will help you to understand yourself better – to develop a sense of awareness of yourself so that you are better equipped to manage others more effectively.

2 **Managing others**: these models will help you to understand others better and so get the best out of them at work and help them to achieve their potential.

Rather than view a model as a set of rules, see it as a set of guidelines or a jumping-off point for thinking about a particular situation you need to manage or a skill you need to develop. Because models are generalised ideas of how things might work, you will need to adapt them to work in your specific circumstances, sometimes taking the best elements from a number of models to resolve a particular issue.

Each tool is described in five standard sections:

- **The big picture**: a description of the model, often including details of its origins and its authors.

- **When to use it**: when the model will work best.

- **How to use it**: how to apply the model at work; how to make it work.

- **The final analysis**: a little more information about the model, sometimes including a critical analysis which will help you to decide whether or not the model is appropriate for your situation.

- **References**: links to printed books and e-books which will give you more detailed information about the model in question.

Some of the ideas may seem obvious on first reading. Rather than dismiss them because they are obvious, think about how you will apply them practically at work. Just because they are simple does not mean they lack value; despite their simplicity, they are a valuable addition to your active management repertoire. In one chapter we distinguish between learning something and learning *about* something. Reading *about* a model helps you to learn about it at an intellectual level. Only through applying it in practice can you truly learn it. If it doesn't work exactly as you had hoped first time, examine how you can make it work better next time.

Do follow the references and read around the topics that particularly interest you.

DEVELOPING YOURSELF

[PART ONE]

Happiness

The US Declaration of Independence states that 'life, liberty and the pursuit of happiness' are inalienable rights and the United Nations has declared 20 March each year as the International Day of Happiness.

A team of researchers at Warwick Business School, led by Economics Professor Andrew Oswald,* says that human happiness has noticeable effects on productivity. You will be invigorated by positive emotions while negative feelings will have the opposite effect. Simply stated, happy people work better.

Whether or not you consider happiness to be a right, here are some models that will help you to become happier and more positive.

*Oswald, A., Proto, E. and Sgroi, D. (2014) 'Happiness and productivity', University of Warwick, UK and IZA, Bonn, Germany.

1 Positive affirmations

The big picture

Many of your beliefs are learned, repeated thought patterns and your subconscious creates behaviours which align with those beliefs. It is worth considering how many of your long-held beliefs really *are* beliefs or simply things that others have repeated to you, or perhaps you have repeated them to yourself over time until they have become ingrained and you don't question them any more. It is likely that some of these long-held beliefs limit your thinking, positivity or actions.

Positive affirmations are positively phrased, short statements deliberately contrived to challenge and ultimately replace your self-limiting or unhelpful beliefs and create positive results. Using positive affirmations forces your subconscious either to reject or to reappraise the very beliefs they challenge. If there is a big gap between the long-held belief and the new affirmation, it will take longer for the positive affirmation to work – rather than experiencing dramatic change, you'll find the old belief being gradually eroded. If the gap is small, you'll find your old belief changing rapidly.

Positive affirmations have their modern origins in the work of Émile Coué de la Châtaigneraie (1857–1926), who wrote *Self Mastery Through Conscious Autosuggestion* in 1922 (and was also the first to describe the placebo effect).

When to use it

Imagine that a belief about your abilities has held you back. You may have said 'I can't do X' as though it were a statement of ability, rather than belief. Deep down, you know that if another human being of similar intelligence can do X, then all that stands between you and achievement of X is self-belief, desire to achieve it and practice! Well-formed positive affirmations change your behaviour. As you tell yourself continually that something is possible, then it begins to seem achievable and you will find yourself graduating towards it, discussing it with others and finding people who can help you to achieve it.

How to use it

Consider an area of your life in which you would like to act or feel differently. Write some statements of what you want, always phrased positively and always in the present tense. It is vital that you use positive language: you get what you focus on and negative statements would simply implant in your mind the image of the very thing you don't want to think about. (Tell yourself not to think of an elephant and you have no choice but to think of an elephant.)

Imagine that you suffer from low self-esteem. Affirmations to boost your self-esteem might be:

- 'I have a great deal to offer myself and other people.'

- 'I feel a strong sense of self-worth.'

- 'When I demonstrate that I believe in myself, other people believe in me too.'

Try looking in the mirror as you make your affirmations. Write the affirmations on a number of cards and scatter the cards around so that you keep encountering them. Write them in your calendar, on your tablet, computer or mobile phone – anywhere you will keep seeing them. State them to yourself with real passion as though you have already achieved them. The higher your emotional state, the more effective your affirmations will be.

Final analysis

Positive affirmations are simple to construct and use. It requires a real desire to change and some self-discipline to put them into practice. Be careful to phrase everything positively to avoid achieving something that you don't want, and always state them in the present tense. The subconscious understands the here and now. 'I will be more aware of others' needs' is not sufficiently specific – it points to an unspecified time in the future. 'I am intensely aware of others' needs' speaks powerfully to the subconscious. Just as you conditioned yourself success-fully with self-limiting beliefs, so you can redirect your brain with repeated positive affirmations.

Reference

Coué, E. (1922) *Self Mastery Through Conscious Autosuggestion.* Digireads.com Publishing, www.digireads.com (the entire book may sometimes be found for free online).

2

Positive mental attitude and content reframing

The big picture

The basic concept is that an optimistic viewpoint attracts positive changes by giving you a sense of control over your life. The more in control you feel, the more you achieve. While much has been written about 'the laws of attraction' and the idea that the universe rewards positive behaviour, the truth is rather simpler: you get what you focus on. If you become obsessed by the idea of making money, you will suddenly become aware of television documentaries, radio broadcasts, newspaper and magazine articles devoted to money; you'll find yourself steering conversations towards money and encounter people with advice to share. All these resources existed before, but you only began to notice them when you became particularly interested in money.

Equally, if you begin to focus on being positive and happy, you'll start to meet people who reflect your attitude back to you, you'll find yourself attracted to those things that make you feel more positive, and you'll seem more approachable to others, so creating a virtuous circle in which your positive attitude creates a positive attitude in others and becomes mutually rewarding.

You can control your thinking, gently pushing away unpleasant or unhelpful thoughts and reminding yourself of all that's good in your world.

Content reframing is a useful tool in developing a more positive outlook. If you get what you focus on, then a 'reframe' enables you to shift your focus. Ask yourself what purpose a negative behaviour may have and how that purpose may be achieved through other means.

When to use it

Rather than considering how you can switch your positivity on and off, think about how you can approach each day in a more positive frame of mind and how you can change your perspective on someone else's errant behaviour.

How to use it

Think of all the things you have told yourself that you cannot do and examine each one in turn. You don't need to discover the sources of your belief that you can't do something; often this is something that is no longer happening and the only things that stop you doing something you want to do are the will to do it and the practice. Consider how it would feel to have achieved something you have long believed you couldn't do. Then take the first step: often this is the most difficult part and once you have begun to do something you will find that it is far easier than you had expected.

Compliment someone when they do something good. Complimenting and encouraging others will boost your own morale.

Express appreciation to yourself for something that you have done well. You don't have to treat yourself (although that might be nice) – just remember to notice your own successes.

Imagine being fired into space in a rocket and looking back down at the earth. The continents and countries seem tiny, and the earth is a small sphere spinning in a vast universe. Now consider how important your problems feel from this position. Any tricks like this which help you to step away from your immediate problems can help to change your perspective and let you see things for what they really are.

Each time you find yourself reacting negatively to your own or others' behaviour, ask yourself the purpose of the behaviour: what caused you or someone else to behave that way, and what could you or they do differently to achieve the same objective, without the negative side effects?

Final analysis

There is a concern among hard-headed business people that management is becoming too soft and 'New Age', and that managers need to develop backbone to be successful. They suspect that self-help techniques such as positive mental attitude prevent managers from seeing the world realistically and understanding that not everything in life and work is positive. Any technique like this needs to be used with some caution. The aim is to check your thoughts and ensure that you are not being hampered by negativity and letting little things get the better of you, while maintaining a realistic outlook on life and a pragmatic view of work.

Reference

Miller, D. (2005) *Positive Mental Attitude Pocketbook.* Alresford, UK: Management Pocketbooks.

[PART TWO]

Memory and recall

As a manager you are a juggler, expected to keep lots of balls in the air at the same time. You can use to-do lists and time-management systems to remind yourself of the tasks you have to perform, but at the same time you are expected to remember names, business plans and other critical information. Most of us have a reasonably good memory; we couldn't function day by day without it. The problem is *recall* – you know that the information is in there somewhere, but you may struggle to retrieve it.

In this part we'll look at some simple and effective ways of memorising information to enhance recall.

3 Loci method

The big picture

[*Locus*: Latin for place; *loci*: places.] Also known as *the memory palace.*

When you need to remember a list or collection of ideas, place each one mentally in a different room of your house and to recall them, take a mental tour of the house. If the list is long and complex, associate each item with a different fixture in a room.

When to use it

Use the loci method to remember any list or sequence, including your to-do list, the key points of a presentation you are going to make or a process whose steps must follow a particular sequence.

How to use it

Imagine walking around your house. Walk from room to room in a specific order. Now write down a list of the things you want to remember. Mentally place each item in a separate room in the house.

Take a mental tour of the house and recall each object you see. Instantly, you recall a simple list because of the associations with each room.

Now picture one specific room – let's say your sitting room. As you walk into it, you may see your sofa, armchair, table, sideboard or lamp. Make an association between each item in your list-to-be-remembered and each item in the room. For example, you want to remember to call your boss about a current project, arrange an appraisal with a team member, call a client to arrange lunch, get your calendar up to date and write a report. Mentally picture the following:

1 Your boss, sprawled on the sofa surrounded with project plans.
2 The team member sitting on the armchair clutching a large, colourful sign saying 'Appraisal!'.
3 Your client, sitting at the table eating lunch.
4 The sideboard covered in torn-out calendar pages.
5 The lamp, illuminating a giant report cover showing the title of the report you want to write.

In the original loci method, objects were simply placed in a particular location. By adding creative images or linking items you increase the chance of recalling your lists. The more often you take the mental journey around your house or room, the longer you will retain the list.

Store different lists in different 'rooms'. Expand the number of locations you can use. For example, you could use landmarks on a favourite journey, rooms at your workplace, even locations on a favourite video game to create different lists.

Final analysis

The loci method is great for short-term recall and with constant repetition is useful for long-term recall. There is a danger that you will confuse new lists with old and you may have to add to your list of locations if you have a number of different lists to recall.

Reference

Smile, L. (2012) *The Memory Palace: Learn anything and everything (starting with Shakespeare and Dickens)* (Faking Smart Book 1) (Kindle edition). Available from: Amazon.com (accessed 12 May 2015).

4 Number/rhyme method

The big picture

In order to remember a list of items, first commit to memory a list of words which rhymes with the numbers one to ten and then associate each item in your new list with the number/rhyme list.

When to use it

The number/rhyme method is useful for quickly committing a list to memory and works best for short-term recall.

How to use it

To use the method, first commit to memory a list of ten words which rhyme with the numbers one to ten. For example:

1 One is a swan.
2 Two is a shoe.
3 Three is a tree.
4 Four is a door.
5 Five is a hive.
6 Six is bricks.
7 Seven is heaven.
8 Eight is a gate.
9 Nine is wine.
10 Ten is a hen.

Visualise each item as you say it and repeat the list to yourself until you naturally picture each item as you say the particular number. Try reversing the numbers and calling them out randomly to test the visual associations.

Now, as you create the list you want to remember, make the most ridiculous associations you can between each new item and each successive item on your remembered list.

Imagine that I am about to go shopping and am thinking of the things I want to buy. As I think of each new item I associate it with the next available number in the list. For example:

1 **Eggs**: imagine a swan laying eggs, huge broken eggs between the swan's wings or a swan carrying a massive egg in its beak.

2 **Milk**: picture your favourite shoes overflowing with milk, the word 'milk' engraved on the top of each shoe or pouring milk from your shoe into your coffee.

Do this for each successive item. Now imagine instead that you need to remember your to-do list for the day:

1 Arrange an appraisal with a team member: imagine an appraisal form impaled on the beak of a swan and the team member sitting on the swan's back as it glides through the office.

2 Arrange lunch with a client: picture yourself and your client at a table, sitting on giant shoes, eating lunch out of your shoes.

Do this for each successive item.

The method is not restricted to recalling just ten items. Combine the rhyming words for numbers greater than ten. For example, 11 is two swans; 23 is a shoe with a tree growing out of it; 32 is a tree with shoes growing from it. Make the first digit the bigger or more predominant image, the second an appendage of the first.

Final analysis

The number-rhyme method is perhaps the easiest memory aid of all. Having committed to memory a single list, which itself is made more memorable through rhyming, you have effectively created a series of hooks on which to hang new ideas. There is a danger, as with the *loci method*, of confusing several lists, but as you become more skilled in remembering associations with the key list, you'll find that you subconsciously create links between items in a single list and fairly effortlessly distinguish between lists.

Reference

O'Brien, D. (2005) *How to Develop a Brilliant Memory Week by Week: 52 proven ways to enhance your memory skills.* London: Watkins Publishing.

[PART THREE]

Motivation

You cannot motivate anyone else, but you can create an environment in which they feel motivated. In 1959, Frederick Herzberg and colleagues* at the University of Pittsburgh distinguished between motivating and 'hygiene' factors at work. Their study flew in the face of received wisdom in declaring, for example, that money is a hygiene factor and not a motivator: below a certain salary level people become demotivated, but above a certain level, money is simply an expected feature of a job and an increase in salary does not motivate them to work better.

While Herzberg looked primarily at functional areas of work, Abraham Maslow and, later, his student William Glasser focused on psychological factors in motivation at work. Their models are used worldwide to explain what drives us both inside and outside work.

*Herzberg, F., Mausner, B. and Snyderman, B.B. (1959) *The Motivation to Work,* 2nd edition. New York: John Wiley.

5 Maslow's hierarchy of needs

The big picture

American psychologist Abraham Maslow (1908–1970) suggested in 1943 that humans have certain basic needs and as each need is fulfilled, so another arises. Starting with physiological/survival needs we progress through a need for safety to requiring a sense of love or belonging, through developing our sense of self-esteem to a realisation of our full potential (described as 'self-actualisation').

The pyramid design (see Figure 5.1), though not part of Maslow's work, has become the standardised way to display the hierarchical model, implying that each level, smaller than its predecessor, is more difficult to achieve.

The model is used worldwide in education, psychology, sociology, training and a variety of other disciplines.

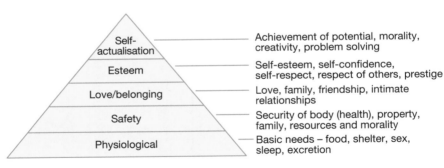

Figure 5.1 Maslow's hierarchy of needs

Source: Maslow, A.H. (1943) 'A theory of human motivation', *Psychological Review,* 50(4): 370–396. This content is in the public domain.

When to use it

Maslow's hierarchy provides a useful starting point for understanding human motivation.

How to use it

Maslow's hierarchy can be used both to help you to determine the sticking points in your own motivation and to ensure that you are creating an environment in which others are motivated. If you accept the hierarchical notion that underlies the model, then it's reasonable to believe that promoting people (esteem needs) is unlikely to create a great sense of motivation in a dirty, unsafe office environment. Get the basic needs right and build on those before attempting to meet the higher needs.

Final analysis

Maslow's model has been hugely influential in shaping our thinking about human motivation. The original five-stage model has been extended by many, including Maslow himself, to include, for example, cognitive needs (knowledge and meaning), aesthetic needs (appreciation of beauty, balance and form) and transcendence needs (helping others to achieve self-actualisation).

The notion of needs as a hierarchy has been criticised by many, including Maslow's student, William Glasser (see below). For as many examples you can find that support the idea of a hierarchy of needs, Maslow's critics will find non-hierarchical examples in which someone has a particular need at one level without having to meet the needs at lower levels.

The model is also somewhat based within the cultural norms of the US – an *individualistic* society – but in *collectivist* societies, the need for acceptance by others may outweigh needs for freedom and individual expression. Apply the model with caution.

Reference

Maslow, A.H. (1943) 'A theory of human motivation', *Psychological Review,* 50(4): 370–396.

6 Glasser's choice theory

The big picture

William Glasser (1925–2013) was a student of Abraham Maslow, and later became an eminent and sometimes controversial psychiatrist. He developed his choice theory out of concern that Maslow's hierarchy was flawed. His research suggests that there are only five drivers of all human behaviour and that they are not, as Maslow suggests, hierarchical. Once we know our own drivers, we can make informed life choices in order to feel happy and motivated.

The five drivers are:

- power and status
- love and belonging
- fun and enjoyment
- freedom
- survival.

Ten axioms underpin the theory, and among them are the following:

- The idea that the only person whose behaviour we can control is our own.
- All long-lasting psychological problems are actually relationship problems (a controversial idea among the psychiatric community because it suggests that drugs are not the answer to psychological disorders).
- All we do is *behave* and although everything that has happened in the past has everything to do with what we are today, we can only satisfy our basic needs right now and plan how we will continue to satisfy them in the future.

According to Glasser, our behaviours are caused not by external factors (an idea which flies in the face of stimulus-response theories) but by the choice to do what satisfies us most at the time.

When to use it

Whenever you feel discontented or unfulfilled, Glasser's choice theory can help you to understand the gaps to be filled and so inform the choices you make to redress the balance.

How to use it

Consider each of the drivers in turn. Survival is the only physiological need here and is a basic human urge. People driven by:

- *power and status* need recognition, achievement and accomplishment;
- *love and belonging* need to feel a sense of love, cooperation or sharing with others;
- *fun and enjoyment* need to laugh and play;
- *freedom* need to be able to make their own choices.

What is missing from your life right now and what could you do to find it? What could you choose to do differently right now to close the gap? Very often a tiny little change will make a big difference.

Remember that you are a whole person, not just someone who fulfils a role at work. If your primary needs are met outside work, it's possible that you will have lesser needs in work. If they are not, then it may be that you rely more on work to provide what is missing outside.

Driver	Motivational ideas
Power and status	Those driven by power and status seek recognition: • Offer them a special responsibility which nobody else in the team has and, importantly, tell the rest of the team. • Give them praise publicly. • Bounce ideas off them which don't actually require their input. For example, tell them that you have been considering a couple of options and would value their thoughts about which is better.
Love and belonging	Those driven by love and belonging are usually great team workers, so: • find them a role that requires them to work with others, either within the same team or in collaboration with others outside the team; • ensure that they always work with other people – they can feel very isolated working alone.

6: GLASSER'S CHOICE THEORY   19

Driver	Motivational ideas
Fun and enjoyment	The person driven by fun and enjoyment may either enjoy socialising, laughing and joking with others and perhaps running the risk of distracting others, or simply derive immense enjoyment from their work. According to the way the driver manifests itself: • get them involved in social events, allow them a few minutes of fun throughout the day (even if it is distracting to others) and it will energise them to work more effectively. If you suppress their natural sense of fun you run the risk of alienating them, so that they have fun during working hours at your expense; • help them to find the things they enjoy most about their work and give them opportunities to work in those areas.
Freedom	This can manifest itself in a number of ways – the need for freedom of thought, freedom of speech, freedom of action. The person driven by freedom is not a natural team worker and thrives in an environment which allows them to work unfettered. • Give them as much autonomy as you can safely offer them. • Give them solo projects – they will relish working alone.

Use the tool not only to find your own drivers but to help others to feel more motivated – see the table.

Remember that the very things you can do to help others to feel motivated may also motivate you.

Final analysis

Glasser's contention that psychological problems are actually relationship problems, and his dismissal of much conventional wisdom around psychiatric practice, alienated many people. At the core is a great message – we can shape our own happiness and motivation through knowing ourselves better and taking control by making the best possible choices in each new situation. Discover your drivers and find those things at work that fulfil them. In turn, you will feel more fulfilled.

Reference

Glasser, W. (1998) *Choice Theory: A new psychology of personal freedom.* New York: HarperCollins.

Pink's model of motivation

7

The big picture

Former US presidential speech writer Daniel H. Pink suggested in his book, *Drive,* that there are just three things that drive us:

1 **Autonomy**: allowing people to control much of what they do and how they do it.

2 **Mastery**: allowing people to develop skills in areas that matter to them.

3 **Purpose**: the desire to contribute to something more enduring and greater than ourselves.

When to use it

Consider this alongside the other motivational theories and pick the one that seems most relevant to the individual you are managing. All these theories are generalisations, and one may work better than another for a specific team member.

How to use it

Look at each of your team members. What are their current levels of expertise at work? What would be the effect if you gave them more freedom to act? Would they relish that freedom or would they continue to come back to you for guidance? Where might you have micro-managed or restricted their freedom to think for themselves and choose the most appropriate approaches to their work?

Has each team member received sufficient formal training, coaching, mentoring or on-the-job training to develop their skills and knowledge? What could you do to help them to develop or develop themselves further?

Do team members understand the strategic requirements of the organisation, the context in which they are expected to deliver? Are their objectives tied to the business plan and is that in turn tied to the strategy? Where there is an obvious cascade from strategy through business plans to individual objectives, individuals tend to be better motivated because they see their own part in the broader plan for the organisation.

Consider each of your team members in turn and reflect on their level of autonomy, skills and knowledge, and sense of purpose weighed against a simple task focus.

Final analysis

Critics of Pink have noted that his book describes no research into motivation between the early 1960s and the publication of the book, and thus it omits several major theories (e.g. Herzberg's motivation–hygiene factors and Victor Vroom's expectancy theory). He does not acknowledge that:

- an individual's needs may change across time;

- needs can be learned or acquired;

- needs vary in importance to the individual;

- motivation serves no purpose if the individual lacks the means or materials to perform;

- regardless of motivation levels, the individual may not be able to achieve the desired performance level;

- 'allowing' people to have freedom to think and develop their skills begs a lot of questions about the management of staff – at what point does the manager liberally 'allow' something to happen and at what point does the individual choose to seek or demonstrate autonomy despite the manager's would-be interventions?

The theory is simple – possibly simplistic – and possibly upside down. Would it not be better to discover a meaningful purpose first, before freely thinking and acting in order to develop the skills to achieve that purpose? It seems unlikely that we master something dear to us only to discover our purpose later.

Reference

Pink, D.H. (2011) *Drive: The surprising truth about what motivates us.* Edinburgh: Canongate Books Ltd.

[PART FOUR]

Personal change

We are limited in the choices that we can make in life by a need to conform to society's expectations and professional codes of behaviour. Yet we often react to situations based on a history of reacting the same way rather than stopping, making a choice and then acting.

Choice, like a dog, needs to be exercised regularly or we slip back into reactive, automatic behaviour. Personal change is not easy, but it is hugely rewarding. The vast number of new self-help books published every year suggests that many of us are striving to improve ourselves.

In this part, you'll find some ways of improving your thinking, discovering more about who you really are and want to be, and becoming more productive through better organisation of your working life.

Cognitive restructuring

8

The big picture

Picture the scene: your boss reviews a piece of your work and makes a number of small criticisms. Rather than rationalise and remember that, in general, your boss is usually complimentary about your work, you take the criticisms to heart, dwell on them and become angry. The irrational response stops you from standing back and putting the criticisms in perspective.

Cognitive restructuring is a process of learning to identify and dispute your irrational thoughts and think differently about a situation or belief. Irrational thoughts appear automatically and we may entertain them, obsess about them or simply dismiss them. If they begin to assume too big a place in our thinking, they can be destructive; cognitive restructuring can help us to minimise their possible damage. It is important to understand that our automatic thoughts are not necessarily our most helpful or rational thoughts.

Cognitive restructuring was first devised by psychologist Albert Ellis in the 1950s and is an element of cognitive behavioural therapy.

When to use it

Use cognitive restructuring whenever an irrational thought occupies too much of your time and you find yourself dwelling on it at the expense of other, more pragmatic or rational thinking. Use it, too, when you are nervous about a meeting or interview, or about speaking in public, or you are simply having a bad day.

How to use it

You can use this technique as a purely mental exercise, but you may find it more useful to write down your thoughts from Step 2 onwards.

Step 1: Calm down

Sit quietly and take a few long, slow, deep breaths. Try meditating (see Chapter 23). It can help to take yourself physically away from the place where your irrational thoughts started.

Step 2: Identify what triggered the negative or irrational thoughts

Write down what happened to trigger your negative or irrational thoughts. Was it something that someone said (or failed to say), a look they gave you, something they did? It is worth considering whether you regularly react in the same way to this and similar triggers. No deep analysis of causes is necessary, but rather an awareness that certain things always seem to elicit a response in you that you would prefer not to have.

Step 3: Beliefs and consequences

What were the negative or irrational thoughts that came into your mind? What do you feel now as a result of whatever triggered these thoughts? Are you, for example, hurt, angry or frustrated?

Step 4: Challenge your automatic thoughts

Now look for evidence to dispute or challenge your automatic thoughts. *Just because you thought and felt something does not make it real.*

Step 5: Find realistic alternative explanations

Perhaps your boss's criticism was designed to help you because your boss cares about your progress; perhaps your boss was having a bad day; perhaps you had rushed the work and not paid sufficient attention to detail; perhaps you had repeated an error which you had discussed before with your boss.

It is important at this stage to distinguish between facts and feelings, to avoid black-and-white thinking and to avoid generalisation based on a specific incident.

Final analysis

The process of cognitive restructuring provides a useful and rational framework to help in coming to terms with the irrational. It is a calming exercise which helps you to step back from an emotional issue and find an objective and rational way to deal with it. To some it may seem cold and clinical and there is a danger that you may suppress genuine and realistic responses to a situation by trying to make everything all right when in reality it is not. Use it with caution and it can help you to maintain a professional response to otherwise emotive situations.

Reference

McMullin, R.E. (2005) *Taking Out Your Mental Trash: A consumer's guide to cognitive restructuring therapy.* New York: W.W. Norton and Company.

9

The Secret/law of attraction (Byrne)

The big picture

Australian TV writer and producer Rhonda Byrne was featured in *Time* magazine's list of 100 people who shape the world, a year after her book *The Secret* became a bestseller in 2006. It claimed that the power of positive thinking is enough to generate life-changing results. Byrne has a huge number of devotees and a large number of critics. She contends that the law of attraction is a natural law of the universe which rewards us with things that match our thoughts, either positive or negative. If we are angry, then events will take place which make us even angrier. If we are happy, then nice things will happen which reinforce that feeling of happiness.

Byrne appears to have been influenced by a number of earlier works, including Charles Haanel's *The Master Key System* (a 24-week correspondence course, originally published in 1912) and Napoleon Hill's *Think and Grow Rich* (1937).

When to use it

Use this method whenever you want to attain or acquire something. For example, you may want to become wealthier, receive a promotion or be recognised for something that you believe you have done well.

How to use it

The method is based on a biblical quote which, interestingly, is also cited in *The Master Key System*: 'And all things, whatsoever ye shall ask in prayer, believing, ye shall receive' (Matthew 21:22). The three steps are:

1 **Ask**: visualise what you want, seeing it clearly and in detail, investing emotion in the request.

2 **Believe**: truly believe that you will be rewarded with the thing you have requested. Imagine that you already have it.

3 **Receive**: be both ready for what you are about to receive and grateful for it.

Final analysis

It is interesting to see a cult develop around a simple idea. In truth, if you focus almost obsessively on something, you tend to do the things you need to do to acquire it – reading around a subject, talking to others about it, changing other priorities to accommodate the very thing you want. Whether or not you believe in the concept of the law of attraction, you will tend to find that if you want something badly enough, you will create the circumstances in which you are more likely to attain it (see Chapter 53).

References

Byrne, R. (2006) *The Secret.* New York: Atria.

Haanel, C.F. (2007) *The Master Key System.* Radford, VA: Merchant Books.

Hill, N. (2007) *Think and Grow Rich.* Radford, VA: Wilder Publications.

10 Seven habits of highly effective people (Covey)

The big picture

Educator, author and speaker Stephen R. Covey (1932–2012) wrote *The 7 Habits of Highly Effective People* based on what he described as 'universal and timeless principles'. To be highly effective, according to Covey, you need to move away from a haphazard approach to life and introduce some self-discipline into both your working and your private life, all based on a set of core values and principles.

The book introduces seven 'imperatives' in three main areas, moving from dependence to independence, interdependence and continuous improvement.

Independence (of self-mastery)

1 **Be proactive**: focus on the things that you can do, rather than wasting time focusing on things outside your control.

2 **Begin with the end in mind**: based on the notion of what you would like people to say at your funeral, consider the end point before embarking on anything.

3 **Put first things first**: start with the things that are urgent and important, move to those that are non-urgent and important, then those that are urgent and non-important and finally those things that are neither urgent nor important. Your planned and prioritised work sits in the non-urgent and important category and you should aim to minimise the list of things that are neither urgent nor important. (It seems odd that putting first things first appears third in Covey's list.)

Interdependence (working with other people)

1 **Think win–win**: aim to develop mutually beneficial relationships.

2 **Seek first to understand, then to be understood**: exercise empathy (the ability to see things from another person's perspective) in your relationships.

3 **Synergise**: find ways to cooperate with other people, even if you don't like them.

Continuous improvement

1 **Sharpen the saw**: do things that 'renew' you, whether physically, emotionally, mentally or spiritually.

When to use it

The seven habits were not designed as a quick fix but as a working philosophy. If you are struggling to focus and organise your working life, then the tools in *7 Habits* may be very useful to you.

How to use it

If you want to achieve something, then you must:

1 Do only what is inside your own area of control.

2 Have a clear idea of the end point.

3 Prioritise.

4 Remember that you must work with other people, maintaining good relationships while seeking your own goal.

5 Be supportive of others.

6 Learn to work with other people, because you cannot operate in isolation from them.

7 Don't neglect your own well-being as you strive to achieve your goals.

Final analysis

At the core of the work are just two simple ideas:

1 Inaction is futile – if you want to achieve something, you have to take action because things won't simply come to you.

2 If you want the action to be effective, you must plan it.

Some Christian writers have criticised Covey (a Mormon) for the fundamental beliefs underlying his work. Others say that Covey's book simply adds to the pile of cult self-help books which may trivialise bigger problems.

The seven habits are not the quick fix that many buying business and self-development books are seeking. Instead, they are about reshaping your way of thinking to become more organised and principled. It is worth considering that putting lots of highly effective people together does not necessarily create equally highly effective businesses.

There are no new ideas here – the seven habits are a rehash of well-publicised ideas – but the book was highly influential, selling more than 25 million copies, and if nothing else attempted to inject ethical thinking into business.

Reference

Covey, S.R. (2004) *The 7 Habits of Highly Effective People.* New York: Simon & Schuster.

[PART FIVE]

Problem solving and decision making

Your team members will look to you for guidance and support and they, like your peers and bosses, will expect you to be adept at problem solving and decision making. Sometimes you have the luxury of time to make a decision or solve a problem and sometimes you will be judged on the speed at which you resolve an issue. Here are some models that will help you, working either alone or with others, to solve problems and make crucial decisions.

Force field analysis

11

The big picture

Whenever an organisation implements change, there will be external and internal forces that can help that change to be effective or hinder it. Psychologist Kurt Lewin's simple model is designed to help you and others to understand and manage driving and restraining forces in times of change. Through an analysis of the helpers and barriers, you can see more clearly where to focus your management effort to make the change successful.

Lewin (1890–1947) contended that, unless the forces driving change outweigh those opposing it, no change will ever take place. The force field analysis can be used in times of change to:

- explore the balance of power;
- identify key stakeholders involved in a change;
- identify acceptors and resistors;
- help in influencing stakeholders.

When to use it

Use the model whenever you are faced with important change, whether at a team level, at departmental level or even at a broader organisational level.

How to use it

1 On a sheet of flipchart paper or whiteboard, draw two wide columns separated by a narrow column. The wide columns should be headed either 'Forces for change' and 'Forces against change' or 'Helpers' and 'Blockers'.

In the narrow column, write something that captures the basic idea of the change, e.g. new finance system; revised production schedule; new time-reporting system; flexible working hours.

2 Brainstorm everything that could assist the change and write the ideas in the 'Helpers' column.

3 Brainstorm everything that could hinder the change and write the ideas in the 'Blockers' column (see Figure 11.1).

4 Attribute weights to the helpers and blockers. Some people use a scoring system, say from 1 to 10, while others use arrows whose lengths denote the relative importance or scale of each helper or blocker (small, medium, large). It may be useful to use green arrows for helpers (symbolically indicating *go*) and red arrows for blockers (symbolically indicating *stop*). The weighting helps to show you where to focus your management efforts, although do exercise care here – a long arrow or high score only indicates the strength of the issue, but sometimes an apparently small issue is a tipping point and as you remove it, so other apparently more serious blockers disappear.

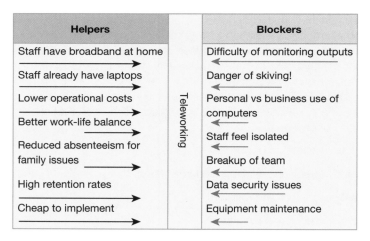

Figure 11.1 Force field analysis

Typically, the force field analysis is used by a central team charged with implementing change. In practice, it is better to explain the concept to those who will be affected by the change and ask them to complete the analysis. That way, you have less work to do in getting them to buy into the change, because they understand early that the change will take place, and they will unearth things that the central team may not know because they are not sufficiently close to the effects of the change.

An added benefit is that one of the most common reasons for change to fail is that those affected by it claim not to have been involved or consulted at the early stages. Using a force field analysis in this way not only involves them from the outset but encourages them to solve the very problems they raise, which is likely to result in a smoother implementation of change.

Final analysis

The force field analysis is a simple but effective tool for beginning the process of managing change. While it is relatively easy to document the forces for change and restraining forces and, indeed, to apply weights to them, do exercise caution in the analysis, which can be highly subjective. Consider allowing those affected by the change to create the analysis themselves, and be open to their ideas.

Note that if you are managing change at work, it is useful to ask those who will be affected by the change to complete a force field analysis over a one- or two-week period, setting out the factors that they believe could help and hinder the change. At the end of the allotted period, they will present you with a comprehensive list of factors to be considered in your change plan. The beauty of this approach is that they cannot later claim that you did not consult them, they will unearth things that you could not know because they are closer to the real effects of the change, and you don't have to work to get them to buy in to the change because as they complete the force field analysis they stop thinking about whether or not the change will go ahead and focus instead on how best to make it work.

Once they have completed the force field analysis, bring them together and as you talk through the helpers and blockers, they will tell you how to capitalise on the helpers and reduce or manage the blockers. It provides one of the simplest yet most powerful tools for change.

Reference

The model is relatively simple and is not the subject of complete books, but it can be found in many books on change.

12

Is/is not problem-solving technique

The big picture

Very often you will be unsure of which elements are relevant to a problem you are trying to solve and which are not. The is/is not matrix is a simple device to help you to focus on the pertinent points and eliminate 'noise' in your thinking. The is/is not matrix is credited to Charles Kepner and Benjamin Tregoe, who established a management consultancy in 1958 in New Jersey and developed a more complex matrix for root-cause analysis. They believed that the end goal in any decision making, rather than to make a perfect choice, is to make the *best possible* choice.

The is/is not matrix asks you to focus on four questions:

- What?
- Where?
- When?
- Extent?

For each question, determine what is and is not the current case. For example, when did the problem appear and when might it have appeared but it did not? What actually happened and what feasibly could have happened that did not? Systematic evaluation of what did and did not happen gives you a complete picture of what is and is not relevant to your problem.

When to use it

Use this method when you need to decide what is in scope and outside the scope of a particular problem or when trying to decide which are the important and unimportant aspects of a problem. Imagine that your team is sometimes highly motivated and productive and sometimes is not. You could use the matrix to help you to create a more motivating environment.

How to use it

Create a template, as shown.

Is/is not template 1

Problem specification:		
	Is	Is not
What?		
Where?		
When?		
Extent?		

Write the problem at the top, then ask yourself as many pertinent questions as you can to ensure that you have isolated everything specific to the problem (the 'Is' column) and are able to rule out anything that at first might have seemed pertinent but is not relevant (the 'Is not' column). Here are some sample questions, which will vary according to the nature of the problem and may raise other questions in their own right:

Is/is not template 2

Problem specification:		
	Is	Is not
What?	What did happen? What specifically is the issue? What parts display the problem?	What did not happen? What similar parts do not display the problem?
Where?	Where did it happen (geographically)? Where on the object in question did it happen?	Where did it not happen (geographically)? Where on the object did it not happen?
When?	When did it happen? When was the first time it happened? When did it happen again? Since when has it happened?	When did it not happen?
Extent?	How extensive was it? How many defects were noted? What trend do you see?	Where might it have happened, but it did not? What possible trend are you not seeing?

You can extend the matrix to capture more useful information:

Is/is not template 3

	Is	Is not	Difference	What changed?	Potential causes
What?					
Where?					
When?					
Extent?					

An analysis of team motivation, for example, might reveal that the team is more productive at certain times of the day, or when given specific types of work, or perhaps based on your level and style of intervention.

Final analysis

This simple matrix, sketched in moments, can save you a great deal of time as it ensures that you focus only on what is relevant and avoid wasting time on false trails.

Reference

Kepner, C.H. and Tregoe, B.B. (1997) *The New Rational Manager.* Princeton, NJ: Princeton Research Press.

Ladder of inference (Argyris)

13

The big picture

It is all too easy when you are under pressure to make decisions hurriedly, reach the wrong conclusions and cause problems as a result. The ladder of inference (see Figure 13.1) describes the unconscious thinking processes that you go through in order to make a decision or decide upon an action. It comes from Harvard Professor Chris Argyris (1923–2013), a leading light in the development of the concept of learning organisations, popularised later by Peter Senge.

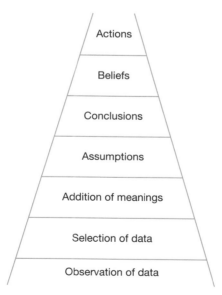

Figure 13.1 Ladder of inference

Source: Adapted from Argyris, C. (1990) *Overcoming Organizational Defenses: Facilitating organizational learning.* Upper Saddle River, NJ: Pearson Education Inc. Reproduced with permission.

Start at the bottom of the ladder and work up.

- **Observation of data**: you observe something happening. For example, one of your team members, Helena, does not contribute in a team meeting.

- **Selection of data**: you now select data from what you have observed. Here you pay attention only to specific data, ignoring other things that have happened. It's possible that Helena was highly attentive to others, listening well, but did not speak in this particular meeting.

- **Addition of meanings**: now you try to explain to yourself what your selected data means. Helena speaks only when she has something to gain from the exposure to the other team members.

- **Assumptions**: you create assumptions based on the meaning you have inferred from the selected data. Helena may be only interested in self-aggrandisement.

- **Conclusions**: the obvious conclusion to draw, based on this assumption, is that Helena is simply not a team player.

- **Beliefs**: based on everything so far, you adopt a belief that Helena is not fit to be a member of the team.

- **Actions**: you stop inviting Helena to contribute to the team, perhaps not including her in future meetings.

There are many dangers here. The first is that, by excluding Helena from meetings, you are giving her fewer opportunities to have contact with the team and therefore she contributes less, so fulfilling your initial beliefs about her. You have created a self-fulfilling prophecy.

The second is that your conclusions and resulting actions are entirely wrong and that you are now mistreating someone based on a distorted perception of them.

The third is that Helena may have been a great contributor to the team in the past and had a good reason not to contribute so actively at this meeting. In overlooking her history, you have generalised based on a specific instance which may have been entirely justifiable, had you given Helena the chance to explain.

When to use it

Use the ladder of inference whenever you find yourself drawing conclusions based on scant evidence.

How to use it

Before you allow yourself to go too far down the path of ill-judged action, stop and quickly work up the ladder, examining your thought processes at each step. Backtrack and find a more considered and rational way to deal with the issue.

- Reflect on your thinking processes.

- Ask pertinent questions of yourself and others.

- Look at history and determine whether the current issue represents a trend or is an isolated instance. This is particularly important – it is easy to generalise based on specific examples.

- Work backwards down the steps from your beliefs and ask yourself how you arrived at this thinking, looking coolly and rationally at the facts and stripping away your emotions.

- Consider whether you could have made a mistake at any level of the ladder and notice the effects that this mistaken thinking may have if you move up the ladder from it.

Final analysis

The ladder of inference is a simple, useful tool in analysing your behaviours. Beware of becoming over-analytical and don't use the tool to rationalise events when an individual is genuinely at fault and needs to be taken to task.

Use it instead as a reality check to ensure that you have analysed a situation in sufficient depth and as rationally as possible before taking appropriate action. Be prepared to admit to yourself, where appropriate, that your analysis of a situation was flawed.

Reference

Many internet articles and web pages are devoted to the ladder of inference.

14

OODA loop

The big picture

When you have to make a decision in a hurry, you need to ensure that it is the right decision. The OODA loop may help. US Air Force Colonel John Boyd (1927–1997) developed the OODA loop for decision making in times of military air combat, but the model has more general business appeal. It has four components – Observe, Orient, Decide, Act – shown in Figure 14.1.

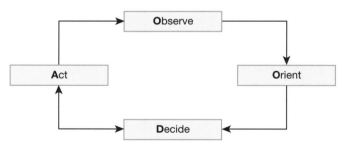

Figure 14.1 OODA loop

When to use it

Use the OODA loop whenever you need to make a decision whose consequences could be far-reaching.

How to use it

- **Observe**: collect as much information as you can from the widest range of sources, including what you see happening right now in relation to the situation.

- **Orient**: interpret the situation, taking care not to let your prejudices skew that interpretation. The better you can understand the reality of a situation, the faster you can make a decision. Boyd contends that there are five main influences on our perceptual filters at the orientation stage – cultural traditions, analysis and synthesis of information, previous experience, new information and genetic heritage – and we must be aware of all of them if we are to make effective decisions. As in so many models, a strong sense of self-awareness is key to its effective implementation.

- **Decide**: every decision is a hypothesis and you must cycle back through the earlier elements of the OODA loop to ensure that you have as much useful information as possible to inform that hypothesis.

- **Act**: test your decision, looping back to ensure that nothing has changed which could affect it or change your hypothesis. This looping back is important – at the time of making a decision it is quite possible that you had all the information available; as new information comes to light, you must re-examine your hypothesis.

Final analysis

The OODA loop is a variant on Edward Deming's Plan, Do, Check, Act model, which brings method to change and problem solving. At one level its components may seem glaringly obvious. Many management models are, but it is when we translate common sense into common practice that we can start to see real benefits. The iterative nature of the model gives comfort that we have checked and double-checked our decision before we take action.

Reference

Because the OODA loop was designed for use in military operations, many of the books that describe the tool have military themes and few focus on it as a management model, despite its obvious applications. If you are interested in the military application of OODA, try:

Ford, D. (2010) *A Vision So Noble: John Boyd, the OODA loop, and America's war on terror*. CreateSpace Independent Publishing Platform (online).

15 Polarity management

The big picture

Polarity management, the brainchild of Barry Johnson, an organisational and leadership development consultant, is a technique based on the idea that what we perceive as problems in which the solution is the polar opposite of the presenting issue are actually just trends to be managed.

So, for example, a manager may perceive that her team members are working too much on an individual basis and the 'solution' is to develop their team skills so that they work more as a team. In reality, both individual work and teamwork bring benefits and problems. Managing the balance between the two is the real answer (see Figure 15.1).

Johnson produced a simple visual tool which allows you to explore all aspects of a problem and see not only the benefits of the most obvious solutions but the possible disadvantages, too. This way you have a richer picture of the issue to be managed.

Figure 15.1 **Polarity management 1**
Source: After Johnson, B. (1996) *Polarity Management: Identifying and managing unsolvable problems.* Amherst, MA: HRD Press. Reproduced with permission.

When to use it

Use this technique whenever your intuitive solution to a problem is the polar opposite of the perceived problem. For example, if people are too individualistic, the solution is to create cohesive teams.

How to use it

Draw a square and divide it into four, labelling the top left and right boxes 'L+' and 'R+' and the bottom left and right, 'L−' and 'R−'. Label the left and right 'poles' of the problem. In the example below, the issue to be resolved is whether to allow the team to do home-based teleworking instead of working in the office. The natural response is to see the problem in L− and the potential benefits of the solution in R+. By completing L+ and R−, you see the complete *structure* of the problem (see Figure 15.2).

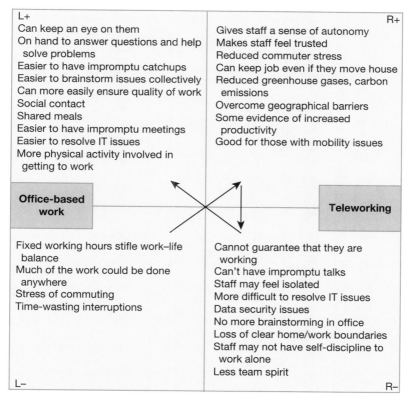

Figure 15.2 Polarity management 2

Source: After Johnson, B. (1996) *Polarity Management: Identifying and managing unsolvable problems.* Amherst, MA: HRD Press. Reproduced with permission.

Now, by stepping from L– to R+, then to R– and L+ and finally back to L–, you see the complete *dynamics* of the problem and the holistic view, which gives you huge insights into how to manage the issue rather than attempt to solve a 'problem'.

Final analysis

Johnson's tool is a wonderfully simple device for ensuring that you manage based on a complete rather than a partial picture. It can be sketched in minutes and ensures that you do not simply manage based on knee-jerk reactions to an issue which is badly thought through. It translates problems into management issues and will help to arm you with information and answers from all perspectives if you are challenged on your management decisions.

Reference

Johnson, B. (1996) *Polarity Management: Identifying and managing unsolvable problems.* Amherst, MA: HRD Press.

Vroom–Yetton–Jago decision model

16

The big picture

You cannot work in isolation from others, but the extent to which you should make a decision alone or involve others can in itself be a difficult decision to make.

The Vroom–Yetton–Jago model was devised by Victor Vroom (Yale School of Management), Philip Yetton (University of New South Wales) and Arthur Jago (University of Missouri). It helps leaders to decide how to make a decision – which leadership style to adopt to achieve the best outcome and the extent to which they should involve other people. While the model was designed for 'leaders', it is equally useful to anyone in a supervisory or management position tasked with decision making.

The model suggests that there are five types of decision, as shown in the table.

Vroom–Yetton–Jago decision model – types of decision

Autocratic decision 1	You make the decision alone, using information which is available to you alone.
Autocratic decision 2	You obtain information from your team and then make the decision alone, based on that information. You may or may not choose to discuss your decision with those who have provided information at your request.
Consultative decision 1	You share the problem with appropriately selected team members individually, gather their ideas and then make the decision alone.
Consultative decision 2	You share the problem with your team collectively, gather their collective input, but then make the decision yourself.
Group decision	You share the problem with your team and you make a decision collectively, based on group consensus.

When to use it

Use the model whenever you are faced with a difficult decision and are unsure of the effects of making that decision alone.

How to use it

Consider the following:

- How important is the quality of this decision?
- How much information do you have in order to make your decision?
- Does the problem have a structure?
- Do you need your team's input in order to implement your decision?
- How will the team react if you make the decision alone?
- Have you shared the organisation's goals with your team and do they accept and share them?
- Could your decision create conflict within the team?

Additionally, you may want to ask:

- Is time a critical factor here? (If yes, then adopt an autocratic approach.)
- Do you want to develop your team members as you implement this decision? (If yes, then adopt a more consultative or participative approach.)

Vroom–Yetton–Jago decision model – leadership styles

Style	Best when . . .
Autocratic	<ul><li>you are working against the clock</li><li>you have the confidence to act without team input</li><li>you are certain that the team will accept your decision</li><li>you have more knowledge, skills or expertise than the team members and so are best placed to make the decision</li><li>it is a mission-critical decision for which you are entirely responsible and accountable</li><li>the decision requires thinking at a level beyond the ability of your team members.</li></ul>

Style	Best when ...
Consultative/ collaborative	• you cannot solve the problem without the input of team members
	• you need buy-in if the implementation of the decision is to succeed
	• the team can help to clarify the problem itself
	• members of the team have more knowledge, skills or expertise than you do
	• the decision is not time-critical
	• the decision-making process could be a bonding exercise for team members
	• the decision-making process could help team members to develop.

While the original model was based on a decision tree, the tree possibly adds complexity rather than simplifying the model. You may find the model in this table easier.

Final analysis

With experience, most managers know when it is appropriate to involve others in the decision-making process and the tool becomes useful when you find that your instinctive solution does not feel right.

Modern management in many cultures has become more collaborative and consultative and you may tend to shy away from a more autocratic approach because it will make you less popular with your team. Be careful here, because sometimes the more directive approach is the more effective and it is easy to be swayed by social pressure to involve others even where that involvement may complicate rather than aid the decision-making process.

The model is designed only to determine 'subordinate' levels of involvement and does not take into account peer involvement and discussions up the hierarchy, which may be more useful than the top-down approach.

Reference

Vroom, V.H. and Yetton, P.W. (1976) *Leadership and Decision Making.* Pittsburgh, PA: University of Pittsburgh Press.

[PART SIX]

Resilience

In the late twentieth century, leaders and managers talked about taking the right course of action, confident that they could predict the results of their actions. In the twenty-first century we think of business as operating in times of uncertainty, ambiguity and paradox. If we cannot so easily predict the outcome of our actions we are going to make mistakes, try things that do not work and sometimes feel that we have failed. Shrinking business cycles, the push for globalisation and the emergence of new economies add to the uncertainty of the business environment. To manage in this changing climate we need to be resilient – to be able to bounce back when things are not working as we had hoped.

17 Kobasa and 'hardiness'

The big picture

Inevitably, there are times when you feel stressed at work, because of pressures within work, from outside work or a combination of the two. Those who are more resistant to stress have been described as 'stress-hardy'. Suzanne Kobasa, an American clinical physiologist, studied patterns of stress in Bell Telephone Company during a restructuring programme in the 1970s and her research suggested that the 'stress-hardy' people displayed three characteristics that made them more resilient:

- **Commitment**: having a real purpose in life (which may or may not be work-related).

- **Control**: those who accepted that they could not be in control of everything but understood that they could choose how to react in situations in which they had little or no control were hardier than those who felt they had no control in situations imposed upon them from the outside and became resigned to their fate.

- **Challenge**: the hardier individuals reframed difficult situations as challenges rather than threats, and saw the potential to learn from new situations rather than worrying about why things should change and the possible impact of those changes.

In summary, those with a 'hardy personality' saw themselves as in control of their environment rather than being controlled by it. Hardy people had fewer days of sickness than others and were less prone to the effects of stress.

When to use it

Use the concept in times of change or disruption at work.

How to use it

There is no quick fix offered here. Let's look at each element of the model in turn:

- **Commitment**: find a passion in life – something that stimulates and energises you outside work. It may be your family, time with friends, a hobby, charitable or church work – anything that makes you feel good. Ideally, it should have little relationship to your day-to-day work, instead giving you something to look forward to when you are not working.

- **Control**: use the spheres of influence model (see Chapter 61) to determine those areas in which you have control or influence and meditation to calm yourself as you begin to feel stressed at work. As you become used to understanding the limits of your control, so you can begin to relax more, safe in the knowledge that you have done everything you can.

- **Challenge**: once you have learned to be calm, you can start to reframe change and new situations as real opportunities. Imagine what you can learn from something you have never done before. Consider, too, that as a manager you are a role model for your team members and the way they see you reacting to change will influence their thinking and behaviour. As they see you energised by change, so you will find it easier to implement change within the team.

Final analysis

Simply knowing the characteristics of 'hardy personalities' does not help you to develop them. It takes a great effort of will to reframe changes imposed upon you as challenges and opportunities.

With practice, you'll discover that events which in the past seemed important diminish in significance and you begin to put things into perspective more quickly. Developing a passion helps you to feel good about yourself, and you'll tend to feel healthier when you are feeling stimulated mentally and emotionally. When you feel well physically, you deal with situations more calmly and this becomes a virtuous circle: the better you feel, the calmer you are, the better you deal with situations, which in turn makes you feel better.

Reference

Maddi, S. and Kobasa, S. (1984) *The Hardy Executive: Health under stress*. Burr Ridge, IL: Irwin Professional Publishing.

[PART SEVEN]

Self-awareness

Since the publication of psychologist Daniel Goleman's *Emotional Intelligence** in the mid-1990s, leaders and managers have been encouraged to develop their emotional intelligence as a key set of skills in understanding and working with others. The cornerstone of emotional intelligence is self-awareness. If you know yourself well and you can determine the differences between your own and others' approaches to work, then you can more easily choose the best ways of working with others by seeing the world from their perspective as you lead or manage them. It all starts with you.

*Goleman, D. (1996) *Emotional Intelligence: Why it can matter more than IQ*. London: Bloomsbury Publishing.

18

360° feedback

The big picture

360° feedback (also known as multi-rater feedback) is a formalised approach to gathering feedback from peers, bosses, direct reports and, in some instances, customer or clients, to offer us the most rounded view of how others perceive us. Typically, 360° feedback is based on agreed competencies. It was first used in business in the 1950s and has gained enormously in popularity since then. It is intended as a development tool, although some argue that it should be used for appraisal, too.

When to use it

360° feedback is a process, not an event. Used well, it should be available at any time for those wanting to develop themselves at work and seen as part of a continuous improvement process. The danger of applying it, like objective setting and appraisals, at fixed dates in the working year is that it becomes a tick-box exercise rather than a development tool designed to encourage high(er) performance.

How to use it

360° feedback works best when the most senior people in the organisation are as open to receiving feedback as those lower in the hierarchy. The culture has to be right for the process to succeed. The process should ensure that raters can indicate not only their scores against specific competencies but also where they have been unable to observe a particular aspect of your work.

There are many commercially available 360° feedback packages. Rather than describe how each of them works (they are broadly similar), let's focus on your role in the process as recipient of the feedback:

1 Identify the most appropriate people to rate your performance. Ensure that you have sufficient raters to make the feedback valid. If numbers are too small, the feedback of a single rater can skew your overall results. A larger number of raters also makes it more difficult for you to identify individuals' feedback, which is useful since the feedback is generally given anonymously.

2 Avoid trying to determine who wrote what. Starting a witch hunt after receiving 360° feedback is missing the point and discredits the process. Raters take time to score you based on observations in order to help you to develop. Don't challenge them with statements you read in your 360° feedback – imagine if they are right and you have got it wrong! Remember, too, that whether or not you agree with others' ratings of you, something in your behaviour has created their perception of you and that perception is their reality.

3 Rather than dismiss or become angry at feedback you don't like, take time to reflect on it. If someone perceives you in a particular way, then something in your behaviour is creating that perception. Use the feedback to examine your behaviour and consider where you can change or improve it.

4 Take note of the positive feedback you receive and make a note to continue to do those things which others perceive positively.

Final analysis

For accuracy of feedback, the rater should have known the individual being evaluated long enough to get past first impressions and not so long that they simply generalise their responses. Some organisations have tried to tie 360° feedback to salary reviews, with disastrous consequences. Two people in line for the same promotion and asked to rate each other may deliberately give each other poor evaluations.

Some organisations use 360° feedback simply because it is seen as the trendy thing to do and it lacks purpose. It should not be a substitute for good management, or for more formal appraisal systems, instead being used as a development tool. Managers need to understand the purpose of 360° feedback and avoid going on witch hunts to track down those who have been critical of them. The recipient of the feedback should own that feedback, not the HR department or the individual's boss.

References

Lepsinger, R. and Lucia, A.D. (2009) *The Art and Science of 360° Feedback,* 2nd edition. Hoboken, NJ: John Wiley & Sons.

Peacock, T. (2007) *The 360 Degree Feedback Pocketbook.* Alresford, UK: Management Pocketbooks.

19 Emotional intelligence

It has been said that the most successful people are high in emotional intelligence (EQ), a combination of self-awareness, social awareness, self-discipline and the ability to relate to others socially.

The big picture

American psychologist Daniel Goleman combined two early models of emotional intelligence to create the best known version, which has four main components: self-awareness, social awareness, self-regulation and relationship management – see Figure 19.1.

Goleman adds *motivation* to these four key components. Anyone perceived as strong in these areas is said to have 'high EQ'.

When to use it

EQ is not something to be switched on and off, but rather something to be developed so that it is permanently 'on'. Where you have effective relationships, the likelihood is that you are already demonstrating strong EQ. In a relationship that is not working well it is useful to examine your attitudes and behaviours through each box in turn and consider what you might do differently that will create a positive difference to that relationship. Don't expect others to change their behaviours towards you, but look at what you can do differently.

How to use it

If you know your strengths, weaknesses, impulses and effect on others (box 1 of Figure 19.1), you can understand how others differ from you and put yourself in

	Self	Others
Awareness	**Self-awareness** How well do I understand my own emotions, behavioural drivers, moods and my effect on other people? To what extent am I able to follow my gut instinct in decision making? 1	**Social awareness** How well do I understand what drives other people to act and feel as they do? 2
Actions	**Self-regulation** To what extent do I control my behaviours, exercise self-control and adapt them appropriately? 3	**Relationship management** How do I use my self-awareness, social awareness and self-regulation in order to develop the best relationships with others, showing empathy, building bonds and communicating effectively? 4

Figure 19.1 Emotional intelligence

Source: After Cherniss, C. and Goleman, D. (eds.) (2001) *The Emotionally Intelligent Workplace: How to select for, measure, and improve emotional intelligence in individuals, groups, and organizations.* San Francisco, CA: Jossey-Bass. Reproduced with permission.

their shoes to understand what drives their behaviour (box 2), then you can adapt your behaviour (box 3) to get the best out of your relationships with others (box 4).

Everything starts with self-awareness. Seek feedback from other people, focus on how your actions and words affect others, get 360° feedback if your organisation allows it and use the other tools in the 'Developing yourself' section of this book to understand yourself better. Rather than try to change too much at once, focus on changing a single habit.

There is an urban myth that developing a new habit takes 21 days, based on observations of plastic surgeon Maxwell Maltz that it took his patients around 21 days to adjust to the results of surgery. In reality, there are too many variables to quantify the time exactly. Work at developing a new habit until you don't have to think about it any more and it has become unconscious and automatic.

Once you begin to understand yourself better, start to really observe other people. It is interesting to note that ritual kills awareness – the more ritualised your life, the less you start to notice. If you take the same journey to work at the same time each day, you will tend to meet the same people when you get to work and have the same, almost scripted, conversations with them. There are many ways in which you can switch off your 'automatic pilot':

- Vary the time at which you start work, so you meet different people on arrival.

- Change your route to work.

- Next time you walk down the main street in your local neighbourhood, look up! At street level are shop fronts and changes to the original architecture. When you look up, you start to notice the history of your neighbourhood.

- Vary the newspapers that you read. Each has its own political/editorial bias and a change will help you to see things from a different perspective.

- Change the news channels that you listen to on the radio or watch on the television, again to see and hear things from a different perspective.

- Try listening to different types of music.

As you start to see and hear things from a different perspective, you will start to notice things about your colleagues that you had not noticed before. As you increase your awareness of others, so you will begin to notice the differences between you and them. If you and a colleague think and act the same way, you have little to do to manage your relationship. The bigger the differences, the more energy you will need to expend to make the relationship work.

As you develop your self-awareness and your awareness of others, so you can start to reflect on what you need to do differently to get the best out of your working relationships. There is an old adage that if you always do what you always did, you will always get what you always got, so if you want to achieve something different, you have to do something different. If you have found yourself in conflict with someone, you may realise that you have ritualised your behaviour with them, having 'scripted' conversations each time you see them. Armed with your new knowledge of where the differences lie in your thinking and theirs, what are the best actions to take to bridge the gap between you?

The self-discipline you show now is vital to the improvement in your relationship. Your relationships with others rely on your understanding of them and your ability to adapt to them, rather than projecting your way of thinking on to others. And everything begins with self-awareness.

Final analysis

Critics claim that emotional intelligence is not a form of intelligence but 'pop psychology'; this notwithstanding, it has spawned a veritable new industry in training and coaching and the label 'high EQ' is worn by many as a badge of honour. The best managers are able to balance empathy with objective and rational behaviour, understanding the world from another's perspective at the same time as understanding the needs of their organisation and providing appropriate management.

Those who are blissfully lacking in self-awareness and struggle to understand others tend to be poor people managers.

Reference

Goleman, D. (1996) *Emotional Intelligence: Why it can matter more than IQ.* London: Bloomsbury Publishing.

Johari window

20

The big picture

The Johari window is a simple tool for understanding what we do and do not know about ourselves and what others do and do not know about us. Whether consciously or unconsciously, we constantly reveal aspects of ourselves to others, and we may also have hidden potential which is obvious neither to us nor to others. The Johari window, named after its originators, Joseph Luft (1916–2014) and Harry Ingham (1914–1995), is a communication model designed to build trust through self-disclosure and feedback from others. It is divided into four quadrants, each representing different combinations of what we and others know about us – see Figure 20.1.

	Known to self	Not known to self
Known to others	**Open/free area** What I know about me that others also know about me 1	**Blind area** What others know about me that I don't know about myself 2
Not known to others	**Hidden area (façade)** What I know about myself that others don't know about me 3	**Unknown area** What neither I nor others know about me 4

Figure 20.1 Johari window

Source: After Luft, J. and Ingham, H. (1955) 'The Johari window: a graphic model of interpersonal awareness', Proceedings of the Western Training Laboratory in Group Development, Los Angeles, CA: UCLA Extension Office.

- **Quadrant 1 – the open area**: teams work most productively when their members know each other well. When you disclose information about yourself, you develop trust. You disclose that information through your behaviours, attitudes, knowledge, skills, experience and the things you say and do. The aim in a productive team is to increase the size of quadrant 1, the open area. This is the area of good communication and trust. Inevitably there are some things that you do not want to reveal to others and you are entitled to your privacy. Expanding quadrant 1 is a matter of judgement and balance.

- **Quadrant 2 – the blind area**: there may be things that others perceive in you of which you are not aware, either because you lack self-awareness or awareness of the messages that you are giving other people, or because you have chosen not to disclose those things. You can reduce the size of this area and increase quadrant 1 by becoming more open, soliciting others' feedback and working to increase your self-awareness.

- **Quadrant 3 – the hidden area**: there may be things you do not want to reveal to others – for example, private feelings, history, biases or prejudices, hidden agendas, fears or bad intentions. You must, of course, be selective in what you reveal to others, and there are some things it is best to keep to yourself. Be careful not to be or to appear secretive or manipulative – it is in this quadrant that mistrust may be generated.

- **Quadrant 4 – the unknown area**: this quadrant represents potential, unexplored feelings, latent abilities and unexplored possibilities. You can explore these areas through coaching, counselling, self-discovery and risk taking.

When to use it

You can use the Johari window to develop your self-awareness, to foster better teamworking and as a coaching tool.

How to use it

To develop your self-awareness, focus on how you communicate with others and what you choose to reveal about yourself. Seek feedback regularly from people you trust and test whether your self-perception matches their perception of you. If it doesn't, treat the feedback as a positive gift of information and examine how your behaviours have shaped the other person's perception of you.

To foster better teamworking, test the feedback you have received from others in quadrant 2 by changing your behaviours where others' perceptions of you have been negative. Has it made a difference? Go back to those who offered the feedback and ask whether they have noticed a difference. Do they now perceive you more positively?

Consider whether you are as open as you could be with your team and your colleagues. You may choose to withhold some things because you feel they would damage your professional integrity. You may be holding on to the notions that knowledge is power and revelation would dilute your power. Are you too closed? Would others react to you better if you opened up a little more? What would you list about yourself in quadrant 3?

Finally, what can you do to exploit your potential? Do you allow self-limiting beliefs to hold you back from areas in which, with practice, you could excel? Do you label yourself and your work roles in ways that limit your thinking and so preclude other possibilities? Do you hesitate to take (managed) risks? Have you ritualised your working life to the extent that you no longer see new opportunities?

The Johari window can be used as a coaching tool to help others to better understand themselves and the effects of their behaviours on the team. You can also use it as the basis for conversation with your coach or mentor, setting goals around safely increasing the size of quadrant 1.

Final analysis

The tool works best when everyone sees some value in feedback and is prepared to accept it as well as give it. You have to be extremely careful about what you choose to disclose; to remain credible as a manager, there may be some things it is better not to discuss. You should be friendly with your team, but you cannot be their friend, and what you disclose can enhance or damage your standing with the team. Once you have disclosed something, you have no control over how that information is passed on to others outside your team.

Using the Johari window as an academic exercise serves no purpose – you have to be prepared to demonstrate willingness to accept feedback and to change accordingly.

Reference

Luft, J. and Ingham, H. (1955) 'The Johari window: a graphic model of interpersonal awareness', Proceedings of the Western Training Laboratory in Group Development, Los Angeles, CA: UCLA Extension Office.

21 Multiple intelligences

The big picture

Standard IQ tests measure numeracy, verbal and non-verbal reasoning and yet many people who would achieve low scores in an IQ test are extremely successful in life. Harvard Professor Howard Gardner's theory of multiple intelligences suggests that there are at least nine forms of intelligence and an understanding of our own can help us make the best choices to be successful.

Gardner's work flew in the face of established thinking about children's development, arguing that a child may at any single time be in very different stages in the development of different 'intelligences'. Gardner initially listed seven 'intelligences' and the list was extended later.

A knowledge of your personal strengths in different areas of intelligence can help you to make informed choices about what to do and areas that you want to develop.

The intelligences are shown in the table (in no specific order and without ranking).

Type of intelligence	Characteristics (Indicative, but note that not everyone possessing a particular type of intelligence will display all of these characteristics)
Linguistic	● Facility to learn other languages. ● Ability to be creative in one's own language. ● Ability to speak articulately (and possibly, publicly).
Musical	● Ability to play an instrument, sing, whistle, hum in tune. ● Deep appreciation of music. ● 'Earworms' – the tune in your head that will not go away. ● Relative or absolute perfect pitch.

Type of intelligence	Characteristics
Logical– mathematical	● Ability to solve problems logically. ● A 'feel' for numbers. ● Ability to solve problems scientifically. ● Ability to reason deductively.
Spatial	● Ability to see and use visual patterns. ● Ability to use an internal map. ● Design ability (e.g. through visual arts, architecture, engineering).
Bodily– kinaesthetic	● Skilled use of the body, e.g. in dancers, athletes, actors, musicians. ● Motor control. ● Use of the body to solve problems (e.g. by the inventor or engineer).
Interpersonal	● Ability to understand the motivations, desires and intentions of others.
Intrapersonal	● Self-awareness. ● Appreciation of one's own feelings, thoughts and behaviours. ● Self-control.
Naturalist	● In tune with nature. ● Nurtures the environment. ● Explores the environment. ● Senses subtle change to their own environment.
Existential	● Concerned with questions of the meaning of life and existence.

Other intelligences suggested but not embraced by Gardner include moral intelligence (ethics, values), spiritual intelligence (religion, theology, mysticism) and bestial (the ability to work with/train animals).

When to use it

Use the theory to understand more about your strengths and areas for development, how you learn and where you find blockages in your ability to learn.

How to use it

Keep a mental (or written) note of the intelligences that you use regularly at work:

● Which come easily?

- Which are more difficult?
  - Are those that are difficult a necessary component of your job?
  - Could you adapt your working methods to use different intelligences to achieve the same ends?
  - What learning or training opportunities are available to you at work which would help you to address the gaps?

While it is not necessary to show expertise in every area of intelligence, be aware of those areas required of you that you find more difficult in practice.

Focus on developing one intelligence at a time. If you are concerned about public speaking (linguistic intelligence), for example, explore training courses, find opportunities to get up and speak, practise as often as possible and ask for feedback from others. Use the other tools in this book to develop your self-awareness, interpersonal and intrapersonal skills.

Final analysis

The focus here has been on understanding and developing your areas of intelligence. Remember, too, to look beyond the obvious as you assess the talents of your team members. Give them opportunities to demonstrate their own intelligences and see what you can offer within the bounds of their role descriptions which will help them to develop their skills further.

References

Gardner, H. (2000) *Intelligence Reframed: Multiple intelligences for the 21st century.* New York: Basic Books.

Gardner, H. (2011) *Frames of Mind: The theory of multiple intelligences.* New York: Basic Books.

[PART EIGHT]

Self-confidence and stress management

If you act confidently, people will treat you as though you are confident and doors will open for you. Aggressive people at work will prey on those who appear to lack confidence. Some people have innate confidence, some build that confidence and some simply pretend to be confident. Your starting point doesn't matter too much – you will be more credible as a manager if others believe that you have confidence (tempered with humility and never spilling over into arrogance).

Work can be hugely stressful and often our reaction to stress is to work even harder. We are at our best when we have sufficient stress to give us a little 'edge', but not so much that it cripples us. In this part you will find some ways of reducing stress and becoming calmer at work.

Anchoring a calm state

The big picture

Russian psychologist Ivan Pavlov (1848–1936) carried out a number of experiments into conditioning of animals. In one experiment he rang a bell each day immediately before feeding his dogs. After several days he rang the bell on its own and the dogs rushed to their food bowl and salivated. He had conditioned them to associate the bell with eating. Many now call this kind of conditioning 'anchoring'. Using a variant of this technique, you can 'trigger' a calm state in yourself in a fraction of a second.

When to use it

Any time you feel tense or stressed, you can instantly create this calm state.

How to use it

1 Think of a small, unobtrusive gesture you can make, which is going to signal to you that you should be calm and confident. An easy one, which nobody else will notice, is a small 'O' made with your first finger and thumb. Now think of a word or phrase that captures the idea of a calm, confident state. You could, for example, choose the word 'calm'.

2 Sit somewhere where you will not be disturbed for a few minutes and close your eyes. Keep your legs uncrossed and your arms unfolded.

3 Think of a situation in which you have always been very calm and confident. It doesn't matter what the situation is, nor how personal it is, just take a few moments to think of it.

4 See in your mind's eye what you saw at the time; imagine hearing what you heard and feeling what you felt. Make the visual image as clear, colourful and vivid as you can, allow the feelings to spread all the way down to the tips of your toes and cycle back down again through the top of your head. Imagine turning up the volume of the sounds until you can see, hear and feel what happened in this situation as though you are back there, reliving it. When the memory is at its strongest – you can see what you saw, hear what you heard and feel what you felt – anchor it by making your physical gesture at exactly the same time as saying your keyword or phrase in your imagination.

5 Open your eyes and break out of the state by thinking of something entirely neutral and unrelated.

6 Repeat the whole exercise. Think either of the same situation in which you were calm and confident, or of a different situation. Imagine it as realistically as you possibly can and when you can see, hear and feel it then anchor it with your word or gesture.

7 Open your eyes and think of something neutral again.

8 Repeat this cycle five or six times.

9 You'll find now that each time you make the little physical gesture and say your key word or phrase in your mind, your whole physiology will change to one of calm and confidence.

10 Use the anchor any time you want to feel calm and confident. As you enter a situation that might otherwise have caused you to feel uncomfortable or stressed, invoke your anchor with your keyword or phrase and your gesture. Nobody else will notice and you will feel instant confidence.

To reinforce the anchor, trigger the calm state as you enter an otherwise stressful situation and then, when you find yourself being calm in that situation, anchor it again.

Final analysis

This is a wonderfully simple, elegant technique to create a sense of calm.

Reference

Rescorla, R.A. (1988) 'Pavlovian conditioning – it's not what you think it is', *American Psychologist,* 43(3), 151–160.

Meditation

The big picture

Within limits, stress can be good for us. A little stress gives us a burst of energy, which can help us to achieve our goals. Too much stress floods our body with chemicals, which may increase the heart rate, the blood pressure and over time cause mental or physical illness.

Meditation is a great way to induce a sense of calm and counter the effects of a stressful lifestyle by focusing your mind entirely on one thought or one area of your body. Meditative practices were documented as long ago as 1,500 BC. There are many methods of meditation and most include breathing practices to induce a calm state, clear the mind of troubling thoughts and eliminate distractions.

When to use it

Ideally, meditate as a preventive rather than a curative measure. Regular, short meditations can be hugely beneficial in preventing you from becoming too stressed at work.

How to use it

Before meditating, stretch your limbs, loosen tight clothing and find a place where you are unlikely to be disturbed.

Here are some sample meditation techniques:

1 Sit in any position that is comfortable, with your back straight. Partially close your eyes (a state known as 'soft focus') and breathe through your nose, noticing the sensation of your breath as it enters and leaves your nostrils. Focus simply on your breathing, as far as possible to the exclusion of everything else. Push any intrusive thoughts gently to one side and return

your focus to your breathing. This simple technique can clear the mind and make you feel refreshed.

2 This is a variant on the first technique. Sit comfortably, with a straight back. Close your eyes and breathe through your nose, first noticing the sensation of your breath as it enters and leaves your nostrils, then turning your attention to each part of your body and how it is affected by your breathing. For example, focus for a while on the way your shoulders rise and fall with each breath, then notice your chest expanding and contracting. Notice the effects of your breath without making any effort to control your breathing.

3 Remember a place that you love and that you find relaxing. Start with the breathing exercise above and then mentally take a journey to your chosen place, imagining as vividly as you can the sounds, the sights, the smells and the feelings that the place induces in you.

4 Choose a calming word or short phrase. As you breathe calmly, repeat the word or phrase silently to cut out other distractions, so that the word or phrase becomes the single focus of your meditation.

Final analysis

There is a wealth of published material about meditation. Once you can induce a calm state in which you are able to acknowledge your thoughts and gently push them away, then read about other methods of meditating.

We are often judged at work on the basis of being *seen* to be doing something. The focus is very much on *doing* rather than *being* and sometimes it is necessary to step away from the pressures of doing to become calm and still for a while. The beauty of meditation is that the techniques can be performed on a train, a tram or a bus, on your commute to work or on a park bench. It doesn't have to take much time out of your day and it takes very little time, with regular practice, to feel the rewards.

References

Chavan, Y. (2014) *Meditation: Meditation for beginners – how to relieve stress, anxiety and depression and return to a state of inner peace and happiness.* Create-Space Independent Publishing Platform (online).

Harrison, E. (1994) *Teach Yourself to Meditate: Over 20 simple exercises for peace, health and clarity of mind.* London: Piatkus.

Kabat-Zinn, J. (2013) *Full Catastrophe Living: How to cope with stress, pain and illness using mindfulness meditation,* revised edition. London: Piatkus.

Mindfulness

24

The big picture

Mindfulness is a meditative technique in which, rather than focusing on your breathing and body, you become aware of the present moment, calmly and non-judgementally observing your thoughts as they drift through your mind. Mindfulness allows you to observe negative thoughts before they escalate into something damaging. It has been said that mindfulness promotes general well-being, enabling you to deal with life more calmly and reducing stress, depression and anxiety.

Though its origins are in centuries-old Buddhist meditation techniques, mindfulness was first brought to the public's attention in the late 1970s by Jon Kabat-Zinn, a molecular biologist, who started a stress-reduction clinic at Massachusetts University Hospital.

Those who practise mindfulness become more acutely aware of the moment they are in. Instead of being hijacked by negative thoughts, they focus on the present moment. Someone going for a 'mindful' walk would be attuned to every little detail of what they see, hear and feel. It is in the little details that they rediscover a sense of peace and wonder.

Instead of constantly rushing through life, doing things, mindfulness encourages you to step back, relax and simply notice what is happening around you and to lose the sense of guilt over wasting time which haunts adults and passes children by.

When to use it

Like meditation, mindfulness is not a one-off remedy for anxiety and stress but a long-term commitment. If you are prone to stress at work, then mindfulness may be the answer.

How to use it

Here are some sample mindfulness exercises:

1 Sit comfortably, with loosened clothing, in a chair that supports your spine and go into soft focus (with your eyes partially closed). Allow any sounds around you to drift into your mind, without labelling the source of the sound. In a sense you are simply being *present* to the sounds around you rather than focusing on any single sound. If you find your mind wandering, don't judge yourself, but simply redirect your focus to the sounds around you.

2 Choose an action that you do automatically, like cleaning your teeth or brushing your hair. Allow that single action to become the focus of your mindful thinking, noticing everything about it in detail, using all five senses – what do you feel as you brush your teeth? What can you smell and taste? What do you see and what do you hear?

3 If you are angry about something, sit comfortably in a supportive chair, breathe calmly, partially close your eyes and then 'face' your anger. For some, the imagined anger manifests itself in words; for others, perhaps a colour or a physical feeling. Don't be concerned if, as you confront your anger, you become a little agitated – this will pass. Now talk to your anger as though it has its own consciousness, asking it to throw what it wants at you, while you will simply sit and observe it. In time you will find you can observe the anger almost dispassionately and without discomfort.

4 Find a small object. It can be anything at all – a natural object such as a leaf or pebble, or a manufactured object. Sitting comfortably, observe the object, becoming aware of the rich palette of its colours, how it is shaped, how it feels in your hand. Imagine its journey from its beginnings as raw materials to its current form. If you find your thoughts drifting away from the object, refocus without judging yourself and notice more.

Combine your mindfulness practice with meditative breathing, so that sometimes your breathing becomes the simple focus of your mindful thinking. Start to become more vividly aware of what is around you, and apply mindful thinking to simple acts to which you generally do not give conscious thought. Walk mindfully. Be mindful of how you talk to others. Be mindful of how you sit and stand. With practice, you will find that your awareness is sharpened in both new and familiar situations.

Final analysis

Any meditative practice conducted on a regular basis will yield benefits. Don't use it to suppress real issues which you need to confront, but to create a sense of calm in which you can more readily deal with those issues.

References

Collar, P. (2014) *The Little Book of Mindfulness: 10 minutes a day to less stress, more peace.* London: Gaia Books.

Kabat-Zinn, J. (2004) *Wherever You Go, There You Are: Mindfulness meditation for everyday life.* London: Piatkus.

Williams, M. and Penman, D. (2011) *Mindfulness: A practical guide to finding peace in a frantic world.* London: Piatkus.

[PART NINE]

Time management, concentration and focus

When you are faced with a huge to-do list, it can be difficult to know where to start. Overwhelmed by the amount of work that you have to do, it's easy to jump from one task to another with no real focus and drifting concentration. You need a healthy balance between work and play and the better your work–life balance, the more productive you will be at work, with less apparent effort, and the happier (and better company) you will be with family and friends outside work.

In this part you will find some key tools for managing your time, and a useful model for assessing and improving your current work–life balance.

25 Covey's time matrix (Eisenhower)

The big picture

Stephen Covey (1932–2012) popularised a tool used by US President Eisenhower, designed to help you to prioritise your time and activities based on the levels of importance and urgency of your tasks – see Figure 25.1.

Think of the quadrants this way:

1 Deadlines and crises.

2 Planned, prioritised work.

3 Disallowable interruptions which you allow anyway.

4 Things that you should probably do outside work.

	Urgent	Not urgent
Important	**1** Crises Pressing problems Deadline-driven projects Deadline-driven meetings	**2** Preparation Planning Prevention PC activities Relationship building Recognising new opportunities Planning Recreation
Not important	**3** Interruptions Some calls Some mail Some reports Some meetings Popular activities	**4** Trivia Busy work Some mail Some phone calls Time-wasters Pleasant activities

Figure 25.1 Covey's time matrix

Source: Adapted from Covey, S.R. (2004) *The 7 Habits of Highly Effective People.* New York: Simon & Schuster. Reproduced with permission.

When to use it

The time matrix is a useful replacement for a standard to-do list.

How to use it

Create a simple 4 × 4 grid on a piece of A4 paper and label it as shown in Figure 25.1. On a separate piece of paper, list everything you need to do, in no particular order. Now work through the list, numbering each item according to the quadrants in the matrix (1 = urgent and important, etc.). Transfer the items from the completed list into the appropriate quadrants in your grid.

Quadrant 2 should contain the longest list. This is the area for your planned, prioritised day-to-day work. If you find too much in quadrant 1, then you are simply fire-fighting and moving from one crisis to another. This is not a healthy way to work. If you find too many pressing deadlines imposed upon you by others, use some of the assertiveness tools in this book to say 'no' and rationalise your workload.

At the end of a working day, plan your activities for the next day. By externalising your plans (i.e. writing them down instead of simply thinking about them), you'll find that you relax better away from work, knowing that you have planned as much as possible.

Work through the items in the matrix one quadrant at a time, starting with quadrant 1, urgent and important.

Often, the items in quadrant 1 are imposed on you by others. For example, your boss will give you a piece of work and tell you it is urgent and must be completed by noon tomorrow. You drop everything and do all in your power to finish the work by the noon deadline. You hand it over to your boss, who says either 'Oh, I hadn't expected that so soon' or 'Leave it on the pile there and I will review it when I have time'. The moment the work was given to you, it moved off the boss's urgent list. Next time someone gives you a piece of work with an urgent deadline, try one of the following tactics:

- Ask, 'Which part of the work is urgent?' Typically, the person giving you the work will be stopped in their tracks by the question and after some thought will tell you that one small piece is urgent. You can now file the rest in quadrant 2, with your planned and prioritised work.

- Say, 'I am happy to do this but this will mean that the other urgent work that we have agreed will be ready a day later.' The trick here is not to ask whether that is okay but simply to state that this is what will happen.

- State that you are happy to do this work and, given that you had already agreed other priorities with your boss, you need to discuss the new priorities. If you are told that this is the highest priority, tell the boss that it will delay your other work by a day. Again, don't ask but state this assertively.

- Finally, explain that you have no spare capacity if you are to meet your other deadlines, but you are prepared to spend a few minutes trying to find someone else with the spare capacity to do the work.

Each of these responses sends a quiet, clear message that you are in control of your work and you are able to manage your priorities.

Check regularly that you are not allowing too much to fall into quadrants 3 and 4. Real life goes on outside work and there will, inevitably, be things you have to do during the working day that are not strictly work-related. Try to manage your time to minimise these items or do them during breaks so that they do not interfere with your work. Put-down and pick-up time when you allow yourself to be distracted from more important work is expensive.

Final analysis

Like any planning tool, the matrix is effective only if you use it and keep it up to date. It will help you plan your time, but it won't help you to do the things you have planned. Good time management is a combination of self-discipline and the ability to say 'no'. Be open to your team members saying 'no' to you, too, and respect their priorities and deadlines.

Reference

Covey, S.R. (2004) *The 7 Habits of Highly Effective People.* New York: Simon & Schuster.

There is also a vast number of articles on the internet devoted to the time matrix.

Getting things done (Allen)

26

The big picture

Management consultant David Allen developed a cult following in the US when he published his ideas on personal organisation. His book, *Getting Things Done,* provided a set of common-sense ideas to use time better. Getting things done (GTD) can help you to streamline your to-dos, tasks, emails, meetings and anything else that is taking up thinking space so that you can become more productive, creative and effective.
The basic steps include:

- Collect
- Process
- Organise
- Review
- Do

When to use it

Those who use GTD have replaced all their other time-management tools with it.

How to use it

GTD requires a big time commitment up front to collect and organise your ideas. It replaces any other time-management system you may be using. In the complete version of GTD, there are tools to manage each stage of the process.

- **Collect**: list everything that has your attention or concern, no matter how big or small. This may come from a physical in-tray, paper-based notes, electronic notes, voice recordings or email. According to Allen, success comes by getting everything out of your head and into a collection 'bucket' (your chosen repository for the collection). You must create the smallest manageable number of collection buckets and you must 'empty' them as often as possible. The emptying process may mean removing it from the collection, deciding how you will deal with it and then doing something with it. This may mean finishing it, organising it better or taking some action towards its completion.

- **Process**: decide what to do with each item listed. As you process each item, consider whether it requires action. If not, throw it away or retain it for later review or reference. If it does and it can be dealt with in two minutes, do it; otherwise, delegate or defer it.

- **Organise**: categorise items in appropriate 'buckets'. The eight standard buckets are trash, someday/maybe (review later), reference, projects, project plans, waiting (for delegated work), calendar (with a specific date allocated) and next actions (do as soon as possible).

- **Review**: frequently review each item that requires action. Allen recommends a weekly review of everything you have collected and organised.

- **Do**: choose the best actions to take, based on context, available time, level of energy available and priority. To organise your daily work, take care of predefined work, do work that shows up on the day and define your work as you go along, so that you take the best action towards achieving it.

GTD also includes a good deal of advice on project planning and reviewing your work.

Final analysis

The essence of GTD is to organise your 'stuff' (as Allen calls it) so you can take action or simply get rid of it.

It is surprising that a time-management system can gain cult status. Perhaps in a busy world we are looking for a wand to wave that will help us make better use of our time, and GTD captured the imagination of many stressed by the apparent lack of organisation in their lives. GTD is not a magic wand and it requires great commitment to use it. If you are prepared to invest time in it, the self-discipline it enforces will have useful spin-off effects in other areas of your working and personal life.

References

Allen, D. (2002) *Getting Things Done: How to achieve stress-free productivity.* London: Piatkus.

Rather ironically, there is a summary of Allen's book for those who don't have time to read the complete book:

Shortcut summaries (2012) *Getting Things Done: A time saving summary of David Allen's book on productivity.* CreateSpace Independent Publishing Platform (online).

Wheel of life

The big picture

A graphical tool to help you to analyse what is important to you in life, and what you need to do to manage your time/work–life balance more effectively. One of the most talked about issues at work is work–life balance and it has been said that organisations discuss it only when they don't have it. It can be easy to lose sight of what is really important to us, to feel indispensable at work and neglect those things that make our life richer. The wheel of life is a simple yet powerful tool that gives you a 'snapshot' of your life and helps you to determine your true priorities. It also shows you what you must let go in order to gain what you really want.

When to use it

If you feel that there is an imbalance between work and home life, if you are considering changing your role or your job, then the wheel of life can be remarkably helpful in putting things into perspective.

How to use it

1 List the eight things that are most important to you to keep your life in balance, e.g. friends, work, family, health, money, etc.

2 Draw a circle and divide it into eight equal segments.

3 Write each item in your list at the head of a 'spoke' in the circle.

4 Imagine a scoring system from 0 (nothing) at the centre of the circle to 10 (as good as it gets) at the outside.

5 Mark your score on each spoke.

6 Join up the lines. How near to a perfect circle? How close to the outside edge? Some elements in the circle will be more important to you than others, so a perfect circle is an unrealistic expectation.

7 Work round the circle again. Look at the low scoring areas. What would a perfect 10 mean for you? Make a statement and write this down. Be specific, e.g. Work: less of it; Money: more of it; Fun: more dancing; etc.

8 Now start at your 12 noon line. Ask yourself: 'If I achieved a perfect 10 for this, how many of these other goals would I reach?' Add 1 point to each of those it would help you to move on.

9 Ask yourself what you would have to reduce or let go of in order to get better scores on the lines that represent the things that are most important to you.

10 Repeat for each item.

Now consider the first steps you will take to improve your scores in the most important areas and reduce the scores in the less important areas.

In the example in Figure 27.1, the individual is getting a great deal from work – it's going well – but is spending little time with their family. Work seems to be giving good opportunities for travelling and reading but little time for anything else. If time with family and friends is really important, then the person must consider how they can reduce their working hours or perhaps adopt more flexible working patterns to improve the Family and Friends scores.

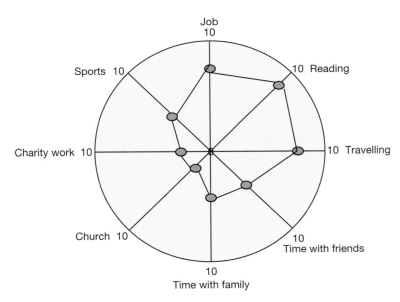

Figure 27.1 Wheel of life

Source: After Paul J. Meyer's Wheel of Life, © Success Motivation International, www.success-motivation.com. Reproduced with permission.

Final analysis

Completing the wheel of life is a highly subjective exercise and you may find that your scores change if you use it two or three times in quick succession. Even so, it will give you relative indicators of what is and is not working for you, and where you need to focus your attention to improve your work–life balance.

Reference

There are many articles on the wheel of life on the internet.

[PART TEN]

Learning

Learning can be a joyful experience – that sudden 'aha!' moment when you make a new connection of ideas or learn something you can apply immediately in your day-to-day work. As a manager, it's important that you keep up with new developments in your field and, indeed, better ways to manage others. Here, you'll find ways of enhancing your experience of learning, and of bringing a childlike sense of playfulness and curiosity back into the learning process.

28 Accelerated learning

The big picture

Accelerated learning offers a potpourri of ideas that can help us to learn more quickly and effectively. British writer, trainer and educational consultant Colin Rose drew together the works of many educational researchers in the 1980s to produce a model which helps to accelerate the learning process. In essence, if you understand your preferred learning styles, you will learn more quickly, embed the learning more deeply and enjoy the learning process more: learning will feel natural.

We take in information through our basic senses – seeing, hearing and feeling – and most of us have a preference for one of these senses. If you can involve more than one sense in the learning process, you increase the level of understanding and recall. You can stimulate those senses through, for example, physical involvement in the learning process, drawing and using music.

When to use it

Accelerated learning is useful any time you are learning something new.

How to use it

Accelerated learning draws on all your senses, where perhaps more traditional learning would use just one, and you can be creative in the ways in which you engage those senses.

Traditional education is something of a consumer process – we are fed knowledge and ideas and receive them largely passively. Accelerated learning encourages you to become proactive in the learning process:

- Turn a set of facts into a poem, song or game.

- Draw a mind map (visual sense), trace your finger along the branches of the map (feeling) and say out loud what you are reading (hearing) – this engages all three sensory channels at the same time and strengthens the mental connections that help to embed learning.

- Imagine the adventure that a writer had while writing a work of non-fiction. Why did they structure the information in this way? Why did they use a particular turn of phrase or adopt a particular style?

- Practise every new skill as soon as you have learned it.

- Distinguish between *learning* something and *learning about* something. Learning about is largely passive; learning is active.

- Break your learning into small, bite-sized chunks, stepping away regularly from the learning process to allow your brain to assimilate what it has learned.

- Learn to make connections, linking new information to existing knowledge and seeing new ideas as different perspectives on old ideas.

- Collaborate with others. One of the best ways to know how much you have learned and understand is to explain it to someone else. The ability to articulate something embeds the learning while uncovering gaps in your knowledge.

- Use metaphor and simile in learning. If you were learning sales techniques, for example, you could liken selling to catching fish. Brainstorm everything you know about catching a fish and then re-associate the fishing ideas with the original concept of selling. You'll start to think, 'Ah! This is just like . . .' and so enhance your learning.

- Measure your progress. Set yourself learning goals and evaluate your progress against them.

- Don't try to do too much at once – learn a new skill by deconstructing it. As you break something down into its component parts, so you can build the skills from the bottom up.

- Contextualise your learning. Abstract concepts may be easy to grasp at first, but without a context they are easily forgotten. Consider where you can apply your new learning in practice and if you have the opportunity, put it into practice as you learn or immediately afterwards.

Final analysis

As children, we learned through play and asking questions. Play involved all the senses. As adults, learning can become more of a sterile, one-dimensional affair based on passive learning, memorisation of facts and regurgitation of information.

Accelerated learning takes us back to childhood – it is sensory-rich and fun. It takes almost no investment of time and the rewards can be seen very quickly.

References

Best, B. (2011) *Accelerated Learning Pocketbook,* 2nd revised edition. Alresford, UK: Teachers' Pocketbooks.

Rose, C. (1985) *Accelerated Learning,* 5th edition. Aylesbury, UK: Accelerated Learning Systems Ltd.

Benziger's thinking styles assessment

29

The big picture

US researcher in psychology Katherine Benziger has produced an assessment tool which determines the quadrant of the brain you use most naturally; using areas outside the preferred quadrant is tiring and may be damaging as it uses 100 per cent more energy than the preferred quadrant. The four quadrants of the brain are described as frontal left, frontal right, basal left and basal right (see Figure 29.1).

Just as we have a preference for using a particular hand, eye or ear, each of us shows a preference for using a particular quadrant of the brain. The functions of each quadrant of the brain are as follows:

Frontal left (Thinking)

- Logic
- Decision making
- Analysis
- Negotiation
- Debate
- Prioritising

Basal left (Sensing)

- Attention to detail
- Routine procedures
- Time management
- Prefers to work with tangible objects

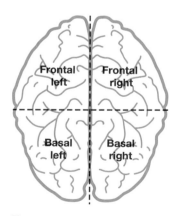

Figure 29.1 Brain quadrants
Source: Adapted from Benziger's thinking styles assessment (BTSA), www.benziger.org/index.html

- Lives in the here and now
- Very productive

Frontal right (Intuition)

- Works with possibilities
- Sees patterns and links seemingly unrelated ideas
- Invents new solutions
- Creativity
- Risk taking
- Humour

Basal right (Feeling)

- Good at reading non-verbal communication
- Likes to promote harmony within a group
- More interested in people aspects of an issue than technical aspects
- Nurturing
- Encouraging
- Creates a sense of belonging

Benziger's thinking styles assessment helps you to determine your dominant brain quadrant so that you can improve your self-management, general working effectiveness and ability to work more collaboratively.

When to use it

Use the tool to understand your preferred brain quadrant so you can focus on finding work that exercises that part of the brain.

How to use it

Whether or not you choose to use the formal Benziger assessment or simply the model of the brain quadrants, re-read the list above and assess which collection of attributes best describes you and your preferred working style. Ask yourself:

- To what extent does your current role allow you to exercise that quadrant?
- How could you adapt your role to encompass more of the attributes within that quadrant?

- When you find yourself in conflict with others, which quadrant of the brain is most exercised? Is that your dominant quadrant? Could you resolve conflict more effectively by focusing on your dominant quadrant, thus using less energy and acting more effectively?

Once you know your preferred quadrant, you can begin to shape your working patterns to use it more and so work more effectively.

Final analysis

Be careful not to focus all your attention on the use of your dominant quadrant. The well-rounded person is flexible and not narrowly focused. An awareness of your preferred style is useful and will explain why you work better in some circumstances than in others, but you cannot entirely shape the working world to fit your preferences – far better to learn and develop the skills that require use of the other quadrants so that you become more adaptable.

Like so many psychometric instruments, the thinking styles assessment is based on the work of Swiss psychiatrist Carl Jung and should be used with some caution. (For example, the Myers–Briggs Type Indicator, also based on Jung's work, claims to determine a subject's unchanging personality type, but up to 75 per cent of those taking the test are given a different 'type' the second time they take the test.) Whether specific working roles attract people who think in a particular way or shape the way in which people think is subject to debate. Treat the thinking styles assessment as a snapshot – the way you prefer to think now – and it will help you to determine how to get the best out of yourself at work.

Reference

Benziger, K. (2103) *The BTSA User Manual 2nd Edition: A guide to the development, validation and use of the Benziger thinking styles assessment.* CreateSpace Independent Publishing Platform (online).

30 Kolb/Honey and Mumford learning styles

Educational theorist David Kolb's model of learning styles describes learning as a four-stage cyclical process which anyone who is learning something can enter at any point. The model, later adapted by psychologist Peter Honey and management developer Alan Mumford, can be used to help you to determine the most effective way to learn something new.

The big picture

David Kolb theorised in the 1970s that the learning process comprises four cyclical stages (see Figure 30.1). You can start at any stage in the learning cycle, but most people will start with *concrete experience*.

- **Concrete experience**: according to Kolb, we do something and the practical, concrete experience of doing it starts the learning process for many. Expressed as: *feeling.*

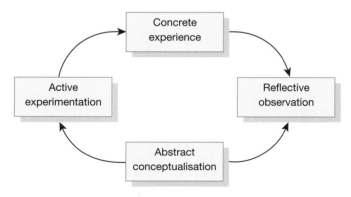

Figure 30.1 Kolb's learning cycle

Source: Adapted from Kolb, D.A. (1983) *Experiential Learning: Experience as the source of learning and development.* Englewood Cliffs, NJ: Prentice Hall, Inc. Reproduced with permission.

- **Reflective observation**: we reflect on what we did and if we can systematically evaluate what we did (good, bad, enjoyed, disliked, could repeat, would want to repeat, can or cannot see a value in it, etc.) then it may move us to the next stage. Expressed as: *watching.*

- **Abstract conceptualisation**: we may start to draw conclusions based on our reflections, read around the subject, discuss it with others until the underlying ideas behind the learning begin to shape the way we will use the learning or apply it again. Expressed as: *thinking.*

- **Active experimentation**: now we start to put into practice the conclusions drawn in the last stage and try something again, which takes us back to the starting point. Expressed as: *doing.*

Kolb acknowledged the very different mindsets needed at each level and believed that each of us, though capable of them all, has a preference for one of the levels. He identified four learning styles which express the preferences – converger, accommodator, diverger and assimilator – and these styles link the elements of the learning cycle (see Figure 30.2).

- **Converger**: uses imagination and innovative thinking, is able to see the practical application of good ideas and is usually good at deductive reasoning – creating logical conclusions from a series of statements. Expressed as: *thinking and doing.*

- **Accommodator**: can be good at finding solutions to specific issues and is often a good project manager. Expressed as: *feeling and doing.*

- **Diverger**: is good at taking a model and using it in a real-life situation. Expressed as: *feeling and watching.*

- **Assimilator**: is good at creating models through inductive reasoning – drawing together ideas which seem to support a specific conclusion. Expressed as: *thinking and watching.*

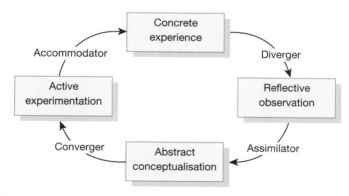

Figure 30.2 Kolb's learning styles

Source: Adapted from Kolb, D.A. (1983) *Experiential Learning: Experience as the source of learning and development.* Englewood Cliffs, NJ: Prentice Hall, Inc. Reproduced with permission.

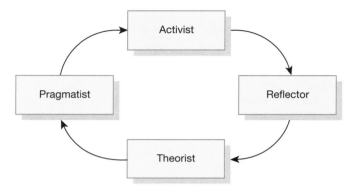

Figure 30.3 Honey and Mumford's learning cycle
Source: After Honey, P. and Mumford, A. (1992) *The Manual of Learning Styles,* 3rd revised ed. Maidenhead, UK: Peter Honey Publications. Reproduced with permission.

Honey and Mumford adapted Kolb's model to appeal more to a non-academic UK audience, and refer to the four stages as activist, reflector, theorist and pragmatist (see Figure 30.3).

Academic studies suggest that three of the four styles map directly back to the Kolb model:

- Pragmatists = Convergers
- Reflectors = Divergers
- Theorists = Assimilators

The activist style, however, does not equate exactly to the accommodator style.

When to use it

Whether you adopt Honey and Mumford's terminology or that of Kolb, use the model to determine your preferred learning styles so that you can select the best learning methods to help you to learn quickly and effectively.

How to use it

Think back to times when you learned something really easily. What made it so easy? Which combination(s) of feeling, thinking, watching and doing did you use? In the table, you'll find the Kolb styles mapped to the most appropriate learning methods for each preferred style.

When you need to learn something new, first explore the learning methods that fit your natural preferences. As your skill or knowledge grows, so you will find it easier to learn from other methods outside your preferred range.

Style	Like	Learn best from
Convergers *Thinking and doing*	To try out ideas in practice	Problem solving Discussion Case studies Interactivity
Accommodators *Feeling and doing*	To be immersed in a difficult (and preferably new) task	Group discussions Role play Competitions Business games
Divergers *Feeling and watching*	Time to think before reaching a conclusion	Presentation of learning from different perspectives Coaching Interviews
Assimilators *Thinking and watching*	Logically structured arguments and ideas	Facts Figures Background information Debates

Kolb produced a learning styles inventory, which is available, for a fee, from the Hay Group, a global management consulting firm (www.haygroup.com).

Final analysis

The problem with any learning theory is that it is just that: a theory. There has been something of a backlash against the application of Kolb's learning cycle in children's education, but at an adult level it is useful in shaping choices about learning methods. Apply it with caution and it can help you to focus on the best starting points in learning something new. Look, too, at the VAK model (see Chapter 42), which can further inform your learning choices.

References

Honey, P. and Mumford, A. (1992) *The Manual of Learning Styles,* 3rd revised edition. London: Peter Honey Publications.

Kolb's original book . . .

Kolb, D.A. (1983) *Experiential Learning: Experience as the source of learning and development.* Englewood Cliffs, NJ: Prentice Hall, Inc.

. . . is out of print and copies are exchanged at many times the cover price of the original book. There are many articles on the internet about his theory.

[PART ELEVEN]

Listening skills

If you are relatively new to a management position, you may feel that you are under pressure to prove yourself. One of the easiest traps to fall into is to talk too much to impress upon people how much you know or how quickly you can solve a problem.

In reality, you will gain more credibility through listening well and asking good questions. If you can talk for 20 per cent of the time and listen for 80 per cent, your credibility will rise far faster than if you reverse these ratios. Listen with attention and speak with intention!

31 Active listening

The big picture

As children we are taught not to interrupt when others are talking and are asked to be quiet and listen. Our brain can process language faster than it can be spoken and so for much of the time when others are talking to us our mind is not engaged. We speak on average around the globe at 150 words per minute (2.5 words per second). If you took a recording of someone speaking your native language, increased the speed but maintained the original pitch, you could understand it as perfectly speeded up to 600 words per minute as you could at the standard spoken rate of 150 wpm. We can find ourselves drifting off on a short mental holiday and not hearing the speaker, or formulating the next thing to say and saying it (interrupting) because we have ample processing time to create our interruptions. This passive listening teaches us little except bad habits.

Sometimes we have a burning question but don't ask it because we are afraid of feeling foolish, thinking that we should know the answer or that others around us already understand the point being made. Again, we learn this skill as children: in school we ask a question and the teacher tells us not to be stupid – we should know the answer because the point has already been explained to us.

Active listening is the art of summarising, paraphrasing, checking our understanding and thus reducing the chances of misunderstanding, ambiguity and partial understanding.

When to use it

Active listening is useful in any situation in which you need information and are in a social or work situation where asking questions is appropriate to the occasion. You may be listening to learn, to gather new information, to develop your understanding of something or for the sheer joy of listening to someone with something interesting to say.

How to use it

1 Look interested. Better still, *be* interested. Be curious about what you can learn from the other person.

2 If you don't like someone, your body language will give them clear messages to that effect. People are more likely to be open and free with information if they trust or like you. Try at least to be neutral about the other person if you don't really like them.

3 Ask probing questions. Never say, 'So what you are trying to say is . . . ' The other person knows what they were trying to say; in fact, they just said it. Turn the statement around and say, 'May I just check my understanding of this?' and then explain in your own terms what you believe you heard. Say, 'That's interesting – could you tell me a little more about that?' Other probing questions may include:

   ● So, what happened after that?

   ● How did you manage that situation?

   ● Who else was involved here and what were their roles?

   ● What was the end result?

4 Tell the other person how interesting their story is. Ask them whether they have encountered similar things elsewhere, or whether they have other, similar experiences to share.

5 React to what the other person has said, rather than creating a new branch in the conversation.

6 Show that you are listening by leaning in slightly towards the speaker, nodding occasionally and making assenting noises.

7 Don't judge what the speaker is saying – listen with real attention and speak with intention (and then only when you have something useful to add).

8 Try listening for 80 per cent of the conversation and speaking for 20 per cent (a useful rule to apply in progress meetings and appraisals of others).

The key in active listening is to show your interest throughout. Most people who enjoy talking about their pet subject will quickly warm to someone who seems genuinely curious about it. There is no more respectful way of behaving than to listen to someone.

Final analysis

You can't lose if you listen actively. You'll engage the speaker, make them trust you and learn as they open up to you. Active listening requires focus and concentration, and increases our attention span.

References

Gibson, J. and Walker, F. (2011) *The Art of Active Listening: How to double your communication skills in 30 days* (Kindle edition). Available from: Amazon.com (accessed 12 May 2015).

Hardman, E. (2012) *Active Listening 101: How to turn down your volume to turn up your communication skills* (Kindle edition). Available from: Amazon.com (accessed 12 May 2015).

Critical listening

32

The big picture

The goal of critical listening is to scrutinise or evaluate what someone else is saying and respond with your own thoughts on the issue. It is easier to listen critically when you have a high level of subject knowledge or a real vested interest in the topic being discussed. Your aim is to evaluate someone else's argument rationally and objectively.

When to use it

Critical listening can be used when:

- you need to understand someone else's viewpoint before making a decision or taking action;

- you need to gather information, separating it from an emotive argument;

- you don't know which side to take in a dispute and need more information before you can make that decision.

How to use it

1 Analyse the speaker's motivation. Why has the speaker chosen to adopt this stance? What is the underlying context that has shaped the speaker's stance?

2 What is the purpose behind what the person is saying? For example, are they trying to convince you, educate or inform you, sell something to you, persuade you to a new viewpoint, change your perspective, or is what they are saying simply self-publicity?

3 How authentic is the message?

4 Are statements supported by evidence? Do supposed conclusions link back to points already raised?

5 What process did the speaker use to gather supporting information?

6 To what extent is the speaker addressing you from an emotional or logical standpoint?

7 What does the speaker have to gain or lose by convincing or failing to convince you of the veracity of their argument?

8 Is the speaker addressing you from a personal standpoint or as the mouthpiece of someone else?

9 How comprehensive is the argument? What was omitted and why? What was included and why?

It is vital that you set aside your prejudices when you listen critically. Equally, you should be critical only in your analysis of the content of the discussion, not of the speaker – it must never become personal. Any response you make to a speaker must address only the content – its structure, logic accuracy, factual basis, etc.

Final analysis

As humans, we all have biases, some conscious and some unconscious. The more you are aware of your own biases, the better you can manage them and so evaluate someone's argument on its own merits, rather than based on the extent to which it tallies with your own thinking.

When you are thinking critically, beware of sounding too harsh in your judgement of the speaker; instead remain calm and rational and model all the behaviours that were the subject of your critical analysis of the speaker.

Reference

Ferrari, B.T. (2012) *Power Listening: Mastering the most critical business skill of all.* New York: Portfolio.

Relationship listening

33

The big picture

Relationship listening is particularly useful in coaching and counselling, when your goal is to offer a sympathetic ear rather than detailed verbal responses. It has three basic components:

1 **Attention**: absolute focus on the other person.

2 **Support**: verbal and non-verbal messages to show that they are your focus.

3 **Empathy**: verbal and non-verbal messages to show your understanding of how they are feeling.

When to use it

Use relationship listening in coaching, counselling and offering pastoral care to a peer or team member. It can be used to build a relationship or consolidate an existing one.

How to use it

● **Attention**: listen with real attention, showing in your body language and responses that the other person is the single focus of your attention. In a busy working environment this can be difficult. Switch off your mobile phone and put it away, and ask not to be disturbed so you are fully present, both physically and mentally, in the discussion.

● **Support**: this means not interrupting, not changing the subject, not diverting the conversation to you, and refraining from acting superior to the other person. If the intention is to focus on the other person, then it isn't about you!

- **Empathy**: listen more than you talk. Empathy is about demonstrating that you understand how someone else feels, even if you don't feel that way yourself. Silence is often more powerful than talking. When you do talk, ask for clarity, acknowledge how the other person is feeling and remain neutral. Your opinions are not important here.

Final analysis

Listening skills require patience and genuine interest in other people. The different categories of listening in this book don't necessarily stand alone. In other words, avoid thinking that if you are 'doing' relationship listening right now, you can't offer an opinion or give advice. Be alert to the other person's needs and be flexible in your approach.

References

Leads, D. (2014) *Be a Phenomenal Listener: Master the key to all effective communication – listening.* CreateSpace Independent Publishing Platform (online).

Nichols, M.P. (2009) *The Lost Art of Listening: How learning to listen can improve relationships.* New York: Guilford Press.

MANAGING
OTHERS

[PART TWELVE]

Assertiveness

There are three general approaches to work:

1 Aggressive – 'Lie down while I kick you.'

2 Passive/submissive – 'While I am lying down, why don't you kick me?'

3 Assertive – 'While I am around, nobody is going to kick anybody, thank you.'

Assertive people believe that they and others have a right to be treated with courtesy and respect, a right to be listened to and a right to be treated fairly. There is a big gap between submissive and assertive behaviour, but often a fine line between assertive and aggressive behaviour. Aggression can be passive (the sulky face, the muttered sarcastic remark) or active (the raised voice, the threatening body language). Assertive people are better liked, more trusted and, ultimately, survive longer in an organisation because they are more flexible in their behaviour.

34 The broken record

The big picture

When you feel attacked or under pressure from others, it's all too easy to become frustrated and respond angrily or aggressively. The broken record is a useful technique for assertively stating your position or your feelings, without becoming embroiled in a verbal fight. The broken record may frustrate others, but it sends a clear message that you know your own mind and that you will not be coerced into doing something that you either cannot do or do not want to do.

When you feel that an injustice has been done, or you want recompense for something that has gone wrong, you can become nervous and find yourself backing down in the face of more assertive (or aggressive) opposition.

When we want to say 'no' to someone, we often find ourselves apologising and adding to our original statement because we lack confidence in our ability to remain calm and assertive. The problem is that each new statement dilutes the original, weakens our argument and makes us sound weak. Others will make us feel guilty or try to deflect us from the original conversation in order to make us agree to something.

The broken record technique is simple – calmly keep repeating your original statement like a record that has stuck in a groove, ignoring any distractions until the other person backs down.

When to use it

Use the broken record technique when:

- you need to say no to someone;
- you want better service;
- you want your money back for something that is faulty;
- you are being blocked from talking to someone in authority;
- someone is refusing to hear what you have to say.

How to use it

1 **Identify your purpose in using the technique**: ensure that you know precisely what you want to achieve.

2 **Make a concise, clear and specific statement**: for example: 'I do not have the time to produce that report today. I will complete it tomorrow'; 'I have a long-standing commitment and will not be able to work late this evening.'

3 **Acknowledge the other person's response and incorporate it into your repeated statement**: 'I understand that you need the report today, but I do not have the time to produce it today'; 'I understand that you are under some pressure right now, but I have a long-standing commitment and will not be able to work late this evening.'

4 **Become more terse in your repeated statements**: 'I can't produce that report today'; 'I cannot work late this evening.'

If the other person tries to sidetrack you, say clearly, 'I am happy to discuss that when we have resolved this' and then repeat your statement.

Speak calmly throughout, and be careful that your body language doesn't give a different message from that given by your voice – for example, avoid big arm gestures or raised eyebrows.

Final analysis

Use the technique with some caution. The aim, ultimately, is to wear the other person down so that they back off and leave you alone, but constant repetition of the same phrase may make them angry and irrational.

Reference

Eggert, M.A. (2011) *The Assertiveness Pocketbook,* 2nd revised edition. Alresford, UK: Management Pocketbooks.

35 Fogging

The big picture

If you find yourself being challenged or verbally intimidated by others, often they simply want a good argument and you are their target. Rather than becoming embroiled in a heated dispute, use fogging, the technique of agreeing with the bare truth of their accusations so that they have nowhere further to go.

Fogging knocks the wind out of the sails of aggressive people and is an easy form of assertive verbal self-defence.

When to use it

When someone accuses you of a particular behaviour, criticises an action or simply seems to want to pick a fight with you and is verbally aggressive.

How to use it

The art of fogging is to:

- Remain calm and show no facial expression.
- Identify the key message – the bare truth – in what the aggressor is saying.
- Agree with the bare truth.

For example:

- Them: 'I see you are still driving that awful old car, then.'
- You: 'Yes, I am still driving that car.'

- Notice that you shouldn't include the critical terms 'awful' and 'old' in your response. Instead, you agree with the basic statement that you continue to drive the same car. The aggressor has nowhere further to go here. They can't say, 'Well, you are!' because you just agreed that you are.
- Them: 'Your desk is such an untidy mess.'
- You: 'Yes, it is untidy.'
- Them: 'Your reports are ridiculously long.'
- You: 'Yes, I do write long [detailed] reports.'

Final analysis

Fogging is a great way to stop an argument before it starts. Typically the aggressor, hearing your response, will mutter under their breath and walk away to bully someone else. The key here is to show that you are not fazed by them and that you will not rise to the bait that they are offering.

References

Lindenfield, G. (2001) *Assert Yourself: Simple steps to getting what you want.* New York: Thorsons.

Smith, M.J. (1975) *When I Say No, I Feel Guilty: How to cope, using the skills of systematic assertive therapy.* New York: Bantam.

[PART THIRTEEN]

Coaching

One of the biggest problems with coaching is its name. Because sports team coaches, who are often very directive, are also said to 'coach' their team members, there is a lot of confusion about the role of the coach at work. Equally, coaching is often confused with mentoring. In its purest sense, good coaching is about helping others to develop themselves, solve problems or make decisions, based on good questions. The good coach does not (as the mentor does) offer advice unless it is specifically sought. Nor does the coach ask leading questions to take the coachee to a specific solution. Instead, the coach asks questions that help the coachee to trawl their personal experience, make connections and ultimately become self-sufficient.

36 CLEAR model (Hawkins)

The big picture

Peter Hawkins, Professor of Leadership at the Henley Business School, UK, developed the CLEAR model in the 1980s as a structure for coaching, which focuses not only on the goal of the coaching but on the relationship between coach and coachee. CLEAR is an acronym for Contracting, Listening, Exploring, Action, Review.

When to use it

Use it as a framework for coaching.

How to use it

- **Contract**: at the start of a coaching relationship, you need to agree the ground rules. These may include the purpose of the coaching, how often you will meet and for how long, the rules of confidentiality – what can and cannot remain private between you and the coachee – and how others can be involved if necessary. The contract need not be formal but is a necessary conversation. It sets expectations and boundaries.

- **Listen**: at this stage, you need to listen actively to the coachee to understand in detail the objective of the coaching session and to help the coachee develop more insight into their current situation. Active listening means checking understanding, summarising, listening equally to what is said and what is not, and asking good questions to ensure mutual understanding.

- **Explore**: there are two elements at this stage – helping the coachee to explore the personal impact of their current situation, and helping them to consider possible options to resolve that situation. Inexperienced coaches tend to jump too quickly to the Act stage, without understanding the coachee's underlying issues. Take time over this stage.

- **Act**: what is the next step for the coachee, based on the options explored in the previous stage? How will they take that step? What will help them to achieve it? What are the barriers that need to be removed to make it possible? Do they need help in removing the barriers and making best use of the helpers? Do they know specifically what to do?

- **Review**: what worked in the session? What could improve future sessions? The Review stage is not about reviewing progress against the issue that is the topic of the coaching but reviewing the effectiveness of the coaching to make it as useful as possible.

Final analysis

CLEAR presents a nice overall framework for coaching and the Contract stage is a useful and necessary addition to the more popular GROW model (see below).

Reference

Hawkins, P. and Smith, N. (2013) *Coaching, Mentoring and Organizational Consultancy: Supervision, skills and development.* Maidenhead, UK: Open University Press.

37 GROW model (Whitmore *et al.*)

The big picture

The GROW model is the most widely used structure for coaching conversations. At its purest level, coaching is about asking good questions in a structured way so that your coachee starts to think, solve problems, make decisions or develop a skill independently of you. Mentors may give advice, but coaches do not. If your role as a coach is to make your coachees think for themselves by considering well-formulated questions, then you need a framework on which to hang these questions so that you avoid loose, unfocused conversations.

The GROW mnemonic suggests the sequence in which you should ask your coachee questions. It stands for:

- **G**oal: What do you want to achieve?

- **R**eality: What is the reality of your current situation?

- **O**ptions: Which choices will help you to achieve the goal?

- **W**ay forward: Which steps will you take towards its achievement?

When to use it

Any time you are coaching a team member, whether formally or informally, the GROW model is a useful device for ensuring that you move at the right speed, never jumping into finding solutions until the coachee understands at a detailed level both the goal itself and the reality of the current situation.

How to use it

Goal

What, specifically, does the coachee want to achieve? What would it look like, feel like, sound like if the goal had been reached, the skill developed or the problem solved? What would the coachee be seeing that she is not seeing now? What would she be hearing from others? How would she feel when she achieves her desired outcome? How would she know she has achieved it? What would happen if she did not achieve it? How would she know she had achieved it? Would partial success be acceptable? How precise is the target? Is there any ambiguity in the statement of the goal?

Many coaches accept the coachee's statement of their goal at face value and so take the coachee down the wrong track. The Goal and Reality stages often merit more discussion than the remaining stages. If the coachee is absolutely clear about the goal and the reality of their current situation, the options and way forward often present themselves quickly and clearly.

Reality

The whole person comes to work, not just the person who occupies a defined role or job description. While the reality of their working circumstances may suggest that a goal is achievable, external circumstances may render it unachievable. Imagine the following scenario:

> Twenty-four-year-old Pierre tells his coach that he wants to study for an MBA through distance learning. He is ambitious to become a director of his organisation and all the directors have MBAs. The average age at which a manager is promoted to director is 34. He explains that the distance learning course he is interested in requires 20 hours of study per week over 3 years. Pierre is currently working around 50 hours per week. The coach asks him about his home life. He is married, with three children under the age of five. It takes little coaching before Pierre opts for a five-year course, starting in 3 years and requiring 12 hours of study per week. Good coaches take time to explore both the reality and the goal.

A thorough exploration of the coachee's current situation will make the creation of options much easier. What would help and hinder the coachee in achieving the goal? What are the other pressures and commitments she faces at the moment, both inside and outside work? What else does she plan which could take time and distract her from the goal? Who can assist her and who is likely to create stumbling blocks?

Options

Having explored the reality of the coachee's situation, you can now work with the coachee to create options which will help her achieve her goal. Create a range of options and don't immediately evaluate them. Brainstorm ideas stimulated by the discussion of the goal and reality. As you talk to the coachee about each option, it will quickly become apparent which ones she favours.

Way forward

Having selected the most appropriate options, get the coachee to break them down into manageable steps to make the goal seem more achievable. What will she commit to and when? Who else needs to be informed? What obstacles need to be removed immediately? What are the obvious big milestones? What will give an immediate sense of achievement and encouragement that the goal is truly achievable? When will you next meet to discuss progress?

Final analysis

There is a tendency among novice coaches to be too helpful. They offer advice where they should be asking questions, they jump too quickly into options and the way forward when the goal and reality are unclear. In a productive coaching session, you may find yourself taking longer to establish the goal and reality than finding options and next steps.

Avoid the temptation to be too helpful too early. Your job is not to find a solution but to help the coach find one. Avoid leading questions which simply take the coachee to an answer that you had already considered. If you know the definitive answer to a coachee's problem from the outset, then you are merely going through an act of coaching when you could simply tell the coachee the answer.

Be careful, too, not to persist in asking questions (because that's pure coaching) when the coachee is becoming increasingly frustrated at an inability to see an answer that is glaringly obvious to you. Sometimes it is best simply to give the answer.

Follow the sequence of questions in the GROW model and move on only when you are convinced that you have exhausted all possibilities at each stage.

Reference

Whitmore, J. (2009) *Coaching for Performance: GROWing human potential and purpose – the principles and practice of coaching and leadership,* 4th revised edition. London and Boston, MA: Nicholas Brealey Publishing.

Solution-focused coaching (OSKAR)

The big picture

Solution-focused coaching models focus on helping the coachee to find solutions to their problems and build on the coachee's strengths. OSKAR is one of the better examples of this approach. Solution-focused coaching was developed by Mark McKergow and Paul Z. Jackson, consultants and speakers, from the 'brief therapy' work of psychotherapists Steve de Shazer and Insoo Kim Berg.

OSKAR stands for:

- **O**utcome
- **S**cale
- **K**now-how
- **A**ffirm and Action
- **R**eview

When to use it

OSKAR works well as a developmental coaching tool, particularly with a coachee who already has some idea of how to achieve a goal.

How to use it

- **Outcome**: establish here the difference that both the coachee and others working with the coachee want to see. Notice that in this model, we look beyond the coachee's own desires and take into account others' views of what and how the coachee might develop.

- **Scale**: how does the coachee rate themselves right now in terms of achievement of the outcome (0–10)? Often the coachee has already begun to work towards the outcome and so scores higher than 0. There is a tendency among coaches to believe that the coaching session must always start at the beginning, but it is highly likely that, by the time you see a coachee with a reasonably well-formed goal, they have already begun to work on it.

- **Know-how**: since, typically, coachees rate themselves at a 3 or higher because they are already partially achieving their goal (and thus have some 'know-how'), at this stage explore with them what they are doing to have achieved this score, so they have something to build on. Remember when you wrote school essays? Staring at a blank piece of paper was quite soul-destroying and often the first paragraph was the most difficult to write. Building on something that has already started is far easier than starting from nothing, even if as part of the process you have to go back and do some rework.

- **Affirm and Action**: here you should affirm the positive qualities that you perceive in the coachee to boost the coachee's confidence and encourage them to continue to achieve their outcome. Actions are little steps built on what the coachee has already done, to take them nearer to achievement of the goal. The fact that you are building on ideas which came from the coachee before the coaching began gives them confidence that they are on the right track.

- **Review**: at this stage, discuss what is better, rather than whether the coachee has attained a finite goal, possibly reusing the scale at the second stage to measure progress. This way, you are constantly encouraging the coachee to feel a sense of achievement, which motivates them towards their end goal.

Final analysis

OSKAR is different in many respects from the more traditional GROW and CLEAR models, and has a sound basis in tried-and-tested therapeutic interventions. It is a very positive method, building on success, and deserves more exposure than it has had to date.

References

Greene, J. and Grant, A.M. (2006) *Solution-focused Coaching: Managing people in a complex world.* London: Chartered Institute of Personnel and Development.

Jackson, P.Z. and McKergow, M. (2006) *The Solutions Focus: Making coaching and change SIMPLE,* 2nd edition. London and Boston, MA: Nicholas Brealey Publishing.

O'Connell, B., Palmer, S. and Williams, H. (2012) *Solution Focused Coaching in Practice.* Hove, UK and New York: Routledge.

[PART FOURTEEN]

Communication

It is said that the biggest problems at work are caused by poor communication or an absence of communication. Good communication is not a single skill but a collection of skills and it is the ability to mix and match elements of that collection that singles out good communicators. To communicate well with others, you need to understand what makes them think and act the way they do and what drives their behaviour. Projecting your way of thinking on to others will yield limited results and may cause antagonism: who is to say that your way of thinking is better?

In this part, you will find a collection of the best communication models, which will help you to understand yourself better, really get under the skin of others so you can understand them and, with practice, vastly improve your ability to communicate effectively.

39 DISC

The big picture

William Moulton Marston (1893–1947) was a polymath – trained in both law and psychology, he also invented a lie detector, helped Universal Studios to make the transition from silent movies to talkies, and created the comic book character *Wonder Woman.* He became very interested in the psychology of the general public rather than in psychological disorders, and devised a simple framework for understanding our behavioural preferences, DISC, which first appeared in Marston's 1928 book *Emotions of Normal People.*

DISC is a tool to help you determine your own and others' preferred ways of behaving, based on the same principles as many of the classic psychometric tests but easier to understand and apply. Knowledge of the DISC principles will help you to understand your communication preferences and to communicate more effectively with others.

In Marston's original version, DISC stood for Dominance, Influence, Stability and Compliance. Others have adapted it, perhaps because they believed the words had unhelpful connotations. Variants include: Dominance, Influence/Inducement, Stability/Steadiness/Submission, Compliance/Conscientiousness/Caution. A colour is associated with each type.

Marston did not copyright the DISC model and it remains in the public domain. This in itself has caused some issues, as publishers disagree about the standard nomenclature and the colours that are assigned to each element of DISC. The most common form is:

- **D**ominance (red)
- **I**nfluence (yellow)
- **S**teadiness (green)
- **C**ompliance (blue)

DISC is based on four 'temperaments' suggested by Carl Jung, a contemporary of Marston: task focused, people focused, extroverted, introverted (see Figure 39.1).

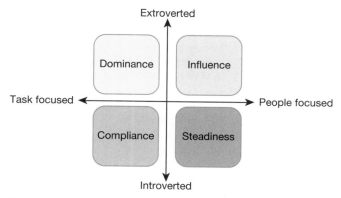

Figure 39.1 DISC

According to the quadrant that most closely represents our preferred style of working, we can predict with some accuracy the types of behaviour expected within that quadrant.

Dominance

For the Dominant person, the focus is on results and achievement. The High D sees people as functionaries or cogs in a machine whose role is to generate results. If a person stands between the High D and success, they may find themselves swatted away like a fly. The biggest fear for a High D is failure and they will do anything to avoid it.

The D enjoys an argument, but an argument for the D is simply a mechanism to achieve an end goal. When the argument is finished, for the High D it is over; the D bears no malice towards an adversary and certainly loses no sleep over the argument.

To others, the D can seem cold and authoritarian. The D is extremely good in a crisis, when quick decisions are needed. It is worth considering that even though the D may not express thoughts about others at work gently, they are an excellent judge of people's strengths and abilities. A D giving direction in a time of crisis fully expects that the delegate can achieve the command given, because the D has already assessed the delegate's ability in that area.

The D is a big picture thinker and, on receiving a report, will look at the executive summary, actions and recommendations, trusting the detail to be correct.

Influence

The High I loves to be the centre of attention, talking a lot, developing relationships and enjoying the company of others. The I is a great influencer, with a basic belief that people are nice and good, and is hugely upset when someone takes action that disproves this belief. The I sees work almost as a by-product of a relationship: 'If I build a strong enough bond with this person, they will be motivated to do the work.'

The biggest fear for an I is rejection. The I is often not a team player, enjoying personal freedom to think, speak and act, so the fear is not of being rejected by the team but more of unpopularity or people saying disparaging or unkind things. The I will work hard to repair relationships after an argument, often being over-generous to the other parties to win them back.

The I can be impulsive, impetuous and sometimes irrational, wanting to impress others and, in so doing, sometimes revealing things about themselves which the less socially oriented types might prefer to conceal. As such, they may be considered indiscreet by the other types.

The I is a big picture thinker and, on receiving a report, will often look first to see if their name is mentioned and if so, in a good light.

Steadiness

The S is the team worker who loves harmony and smooth sailing. The S is a great arbitrator in times of conflict and the desire to mediate is born of a deep-seated dislike of conflict. The S is supportive, collaborative and wants to work closely with others. The S may see the I as a show-off – someone who wants to stand out from the crowd. The S has no such desire. At the extremes the S, being highly inclusive, can reduce the team's pace to that of its slowest member. The biggest fear for the S is change. The S is most likely to have difficulties with the D, seeing the D as bombastic and bullying and most likely to implement changes to the S's life without thinking through the personal consequences.

The S is kind and considerate, patient and a good listener, with high empathy and strong powers of concentration. The High S often has a reasonably high C profile, too.

The S is a detail thinker and, on receiving a report, will often look first of all to see whether it recommends changes that will have effects on their working life.

Compliance

The C loves data, knowledge, research, analysis and information. Cs argue their case on the basis of well-researched facts. They are methodical, reflective and highly detailed in their approach. The biggest fear for the C is to be told that they are wrong. They often form strong alliances with the highly inclusive (and also introverted) Ss.

The C does not respond well to pressure, taking evasive action or sometimes ignoring problems in the hope that they will go away. The C is rule-driven and will often have a strong personal code of ethics or life-governing rules. Just as the Ds like to control, the Cs also have a strong controlling element. Theirs is manifested through rules and procedures rather than directive behaviour. Note that an unhappy C can sometimes behave like a D.

The C is a detail thinker and, on receiving a report, will tend to read the entire thing, ensuring that the analysis is correct, that conclusions actually conclude something stated in the report and that there is factual accuracy throughout.

When to use it

DISC is an all-purpose communication tool. Its application will help you in any encounters with others, whether face to face, by telephone or via email.

How to use it

DISC is an easy to understand, 'quick and dirty' way to assess someone's thinking and behavioural preferences so that you can adapt your communication style to theirs and thus get more from the relationship.

First, consider whether the person appears more extrovert or introvert, being careful not to confuse introversion with shyness. Extroverts seem to derive their energy from other people and introverts recharge their batteries in silent reflection. Extroverts understand their own thinking better as they articulate it to others, where introverts reflect on what they want to say before they articulate it.

Now consider whether the person is more task focused or people focused. Task-focused types are intent on achievement and people are merely helpers or hindrances in that process. People-focused types build relationships to get jobs done.

The combinations of task/people and extrovert/introvert will tell you in which quadrant someone's thinking preferences and behaviours are likely to be rooted.

You cannot expect anyone to adapt their style of behaviour to yours and so you must be the flexible one, putting yourself in someone else's shoes and seeing the world from their perspective, no matter how alien or uncomfortable that may feel. If you are talking to a High D, in that moment you must become a D and talk and act, if not exactly like they would, at least in a way that they would readily respond to.

Imagine the scene – High D boss is talking to High C team member:

D: 'Will it work?'
C: 'It's not as straightforward as that – let me explain some of my background thinking and then I can explain which aspects will and will not work as we want.'
D: 'I didn't ask for a dissertation, I asked if it would work.'
C: 'As I explained, it is not as black and white as that. There are subtleties involved here, and if you will give me time to explain, it will become clearer where we should focus our effort.'

In a nearby office, a High D boss is talking to a High I team member:

D: 'Will it work?'
I: 'Hi, how did your son do in his swimming race at the weekend?'
D: 'Well, he won, of course. Now let's get down to business.'
I: 'How old is he now? Nine?'
D: 'Eleven. Now can we please get to the point of this meeting?'
I: 'Eleven? I'm amazed! It only seems like weeks since you brought him to the "Bring your son to work day".'

The mismatch of styles is obvious. Here are some hints on communicating with each type.

Dominant

- Speak clearly and concisely.

- Don't apologise for the messages you are delivering.

- Minimise small talk.

- Don't interrupt.

- Don't take things personally – their focus is not on you but on achieving results.

- Be quick: they do not like long meetings.

- Focus only on the topic of discussion.

- Talk about what each of you will do individually, rather than referring to yourselves as a more team-like 'we'.

Influence

- Make small talk.

- Talk about people's involvement in the work you are discussing (be careful to be discreet here).

- Use language creatively.

- Use humour.

- Occasionally flatter them.

- Be prepared to meet over a coffee or drink.

Steadiness

- Talk about 'we', being as inclusive as you can in your conversation.

- Handle discussions about change sensitively.

- Stress collaborative working methods.

- Speak gently.

- Be patient and listen well.

- Discuss how you can assist each other in your/their work.

Compliance

- Minimise small talk.

- Focus on facts.

- Make them feel good about their research and knowledge.

- Be prepared to listen to detail, so give time to the conversation.

- Let them choose where to meet (usually the office).

- Talk about quality and standards.

Final analysis

DISC is simpler to understand than more detailed psychometric instruments and very easy to use as a 'quick and dirty' predictor of behavioural patterns. The beauty of it is that it provides a simple language to discuss behaviours. We are all complex creatures and we don't fit neatly into four boxes, but start by analysing your own preferences, determining what takes most and least energy for you, and then look at the differences between you and others and you'll find it a powerful guide to how to work effectively with others.

References

Rosenberg, M. and Solvert, D. (2012) *Taking Flight! Master the DISC styles to transform your career, your relationships . . . your life.* Harlow, UK: Financial Times/Prentice Hall.

Straw, J. (2002) *The 4-Dimensional Manager: DiSC strategies for managing different people in the best ways.* San Francisco, CA: Berrett-Koehler.

Sugerman, J. (2011) *The 8 Dimensions of Leadership: DiSC strategies for becoming a better leader.* San Francisco, CA: Berrett-Koehler.

40

Matching and mirroring

The big picture

We naturally fall into step with people we like, mirroring aspects of their body language and tonality. Because we like people who are like us, this subtle matching sends out signals to say, 'I'm like you – you're like me.' If we do not like someone, quite naturally we mismatch their body language and tonality, and subconsciously we register the differences between ourselves and them. The message is, 'I'm not like you and I don't like you.' It becomes even more important with people we are not comfortable with to mirror them and quickly establish a sense of rapport with them.

When to use it

Use with anyone if you want to develop a relationship, create trust, persuade or influence them.

How to use it

Two people in rapport appear to do a little dance with each other. One shifts their body position and the other follows, one changes the voice tone and the other subconsciously mimics it. This mirroring process is entirely natural in two people in rapport.

If you meet someone for the first time, or are meeting someone with whom you do not immediately feel comfortable, try mirroring their body language for a few minutes. As they change their posture or gestures, subtly change yours to match. Be careful, though – if they become aware that you are copying their body language, it will break, rather than create, rapport. The trick here is to do whatever the other person is doing on a smaller or larger scale. In other words, if their legs are crossed, cross your ankles; if their wrists are crossed, fold your arms. They will not be consciously aware that you are mirroring them, but at a subconscious level your smaller or larger gestures will be interpreted as matching gestures.

You can mirror other things, too: for example, match the tonality of the voice – the inflection, modulation and tempo. (Don't match their accent – it could be considered offensive!) Mirror facial gestures, and play back some of the words that the other person uses.

The most profound way to send rapport-building signals is to breathe in time with the other person. After love-making, people breathe in time with each other, sometimes for 30 seconds to a minute. If as a by-product of the most intimate act, we breathe together, then the quickest way to establish rapport is to match the other person's breathing. As they are talking they are breathing out. As they breathe in, their shoulders will rise.

Mirroring is picked up at a subconscious level. Observe two people talking in a public place. If one always leads and the other always follows, it indicates that each sees the first as the more dominant one in the relationship. If one leads and the second one follows, then the second one leads and the first follows, it indicates a feeling of equality in the relationship. Try mirroring someone for a few minutes and then change your posture. If they change theirs to match you, at that moment a sense of trust has been established and you can use that moment to make your point, set out your argument or establish your feelings about something. You will find the other person more receptive at the point at which they mirror you.

Final analysis

Books on body language will tell you that you can take a single gesture and derive universal meaning from it. Someone sitting with arms folded and legs crossed is said to be defensive or protective. This may well be true. Equally, they may be cold, have a sore arm, which they are nursing, or simply be comfortable in that position.

The important thing with body language is to notice *changes* in posture or gesture, which tend to signal a change in emotional state. If someone is sitting with arms folded and legs crossed and having a perfectly pleasant conversation with you, then you have no need for concern. If, suddenly, they uncross their legs, unfold their arms and lean in towards you, then it's likely that something just changed at an emotional or psychological level. It's the changes that count. Don't be afraid to cross your legs or fold your arms in mirroring someone else – you are not signalling a defensive attitude but sending out rapport-building signals, which will work to strengthen the relationship.

References

McCartney, T. and McCartney, K. (2014) *The NLP Practitioner: A practitioner's toolkit.* Lulu.com: Lulu Publishing Services.

O'Connor, J. and Seymour, J. (2003) *Introducing NLP: Neuro-Linguistic Programming.* New York: Thorsons.

41

Storytelling

The big picture

Business is serious, isn't it? To convey how serious we are about that business, we talk about data and information in rational, unemotive language, thus illustrating both our mastery of our domain and our professional credibility. We act as though the important thing in business communication is to convey facts and data so that people will base their actions and decisions around them – and it's simply not enough! The truth is, business language is boring and it doesn't engage.

If we can introduce rich language, metaphor, stories of our good and bad experiences, stories that disclose something about us, stories that highlight business imperatives, we gain professional credibility, reach more people, engage them at a deeper level in understanding, educate and inform them in ways that embed learning, and enhance recall.

The tradition of storytelling predates the written word. It is an intimate tradition, creating a bond between storyteller and audience. At tense moments in a story, the listener's brain releases cortisol to reduce stress levels; at touching or emotional moments, it releases oxytocin, increasingly associated with relaxation, trust and psychological stability. Stories affect the physiology and psychology of the listener in more varied and deeper ways than the recitation of facts and figures and, when we have an emotional involvement, we remember more, make better connections and the memories stay with us.

Think back to stories you remember from your childhood. You may have been frightened, entranced, even disgusted by them, but even now they still have some resonance with you.

Storytelling is becoming increasingly common in business. You have only to see the incredible popularity of the 'TED: Ideas worth spreading' movement to realise how people are becoming gripped by stories that have relevance for them at a deeper level than dry, dusty business talk.

There is an art to storytelling and mastery of the art can enhance your standing as a professional manager. Gustav Freytag, a nineteenth-century German novelist,

Figure 41.1 Freytag's pyramid

Source: Freytag, G. (1863) *Die Technik des Dramas*. Stuttgart: S. Hirzel.

analysed the structure of successful stories and sketched them in 1863 as a pyramid (see Figure 41.1).

- **Exposition**: scene setting and introduction of characters.

- **Inciting incident** (also known as 'complication'): something happens to begin the action.

- **Rising action**: the action increases and rises to a peak.

- **Climax**: the action reaches its climax or highest point of tension.

- **Falling action**: events are triggered by the climax as we move towards the end of the story.

- **Resolution**: the main problem or conflict is resolved for or by the main protagonist(s).

- **Dénouement**: outstanding mysteries are explained, loose threads are tied together and sometimes something is left unexplained as a precursor to a sequel or to leave the reader guessing.

Whether or not you choose to follow a classic model of plot development or to introduce a two-line anecdote into business conversation, a good story will convey far more than modern business-speak.

When to use it

Stories can be woven into almost any conversation: to disclose something about yourself, to engage others in a business idea, to inform and educate, to solve problems, to sell ideas or products, or to help others to focus on the important things at work.

How to use it

Here is a small selection of ideas of how to use stories according to situation.

Disclosure through stories

You are new to the team and your team members don't yet know you well. Your CV conveys basic factual information but tells them little about the real you. Good stories, which illustrate some of your experiences, can bring you to life in their eyes as a real person, rather than a name on a page. Use stories to illustrate your vulnerability and humility, too. A well-judged, self-deprecating story can do much to present the human face and make you more 'real' to your team.

Engagement through stories

You are about to begin a new project or assignment with your team. Relate anecdotes about similar projects to inspire and motivate, to warn them of potential risks, to help to contextualise the current project.

Education through stories

Storytelling speaks to our imaginative, creative side, helping the listener to visualise something beyond the immediately apparent. Stories integrate perceptions, emotions, ideas, facts and consequences in a single coherent package, and because the story engages a number of senses, it embeds its message deeper than simple recitation of facts and works across a variety of learning styles.

Imagine that your team is frustrated because their hard work does not seem to be making the impact they had hoped. They want to see immediate results and you need to help them to play the long game, realising that, little by little, they are making a difference and over time that difference will be realised by others. Try a simple story like this:

> A freak tide had washed thousands of starfish on to a beach. A small boy was carefully picking up the starfish, one at a time, and placing them back in the water. A man who was passing by asked the boy what he was doing. 'I'm rescuing these starfish,' said the boy. 'But there are so many,' said the man, 'that you can't make a difference.' The small boy picked up another starfish, placed it carefully in the sea, reflected for a second and said to the man: 'Well, I just made a difference to that one.'

Using metaphor to solve problems

To create a problem-solving metaphor:

1 Think of a similar but unrelated problem – a metaphorical problem.

2 Brainstorm solutions to the metaphorical problem, ignoring the original problem for now.

3 Associate the solutions to the metaphorical problem with the original problem, thus generating creative solutions to the original problem.

For example, your problem is how to motivate your staff to produce more work and to a better standard. In stage 1, metaphorically, you might consider how to help your bees to produce more honey and of a better quality.

When creating a metaphor, change the nouns (staff –> bees; work –> honey) and the verbs (motivate –> help), maintaining at least some similarity between the verbs or the next stages will be more difficult.

In stage 2, brainstorm every way you might consider helping bees to produce more honey:

- Give them a new hive.
- Move the hive nearer to the best flowers.
- Plant or grow more flowers nearby.
- Introduce more bees to the hive.
- Split the hive and move half the bees to a new one.
- Ensure you have the best honey-producing bees.
- Protect the bees from predators and diseases.
- Replace the queen bee.
- Ensure the hive is properly ventilated.
- Ensure the bees have sufficient food in the winter months.

In stage 3, map the ideas from the brainstorming problem back to the original problem, as shown in the table.

Help my bees to produce more honey and of a better quality	Motivate staff to produce more work and to a better standard
Give them a new hive.	Move the team into a new office or work area. Give them new, updated equipment.
Move the hive nearer to the best flowers.	Move them closer to colleagues in other teams. Move people working on similar projects closer together in the work space.
Plant or grow more flowers nearby.	Give the team more challenging work. Give the more able members more autonomy.
Introduce more bees to the hive.	Bring in new, highly experienced staff to help the less experienced staff in the current team.
Split the hive and move half the bees to a new one.	Create smaller, more tightly managed sub-teams.
Ensure you have the best honey-producing bees.	Introduce appropriate training, coaching, mentoring, on-the-job learning, secondments.
Protect the bees from predators and diseases.	Remove any barriers to effective and efficient working, represent the team at meetings to free up their time to work more productively.

Help my bees to produce more honey and of a better quality	Motivate staff to produce more work and to a better standard
Replace the queen bee.	Bring in new team leaders, micro-manage less.
Ensure the hive is properly ventilated.	Improve the office environment.
Ensure the bees have sufficient food in the winter months.	Give them stretching objectives, find them meaningful work even at times when they are not stretched.

When you try to brainstorm a problem, you bring along all the prior knowledge of that issue and it restricts your thinking. When you brainstorm a metaphorical problem you are freed from the constraining knowledge or beliefs attached to the original issue.

Selling products and ideas through stories

There are four basic approaches to influencing others, as shown in Figure 41.2.

In selling products or ideas, put yourself in the shoes of the person you want to influence. How do they speak to you? Do they position their own arguments or needs on the basis of pure facts and rational discussion (head) or a more emotional stance (heart)? Create your story accordingly.

Let's say you are a travel agent trying to sell a holiday to a love-struck young couple:

Imagine standing on the pure white sands of the beach, the sea lapping at your feet, hardly a cloud in the clear, blue sky . . . (Heart/Pull)

Your next customers are on a tight budget, simply looking for a holiday that they can afford:

There are just three holidays in your price range: a city break in Prague, a long weekend skiing in Austria or a five-day unguided cycle trip along the Loire. All the other holidays are, unfortunately, out of your price range. (Head/Push)

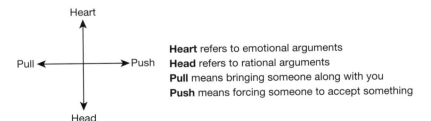

Figure 41.2 Influencing model

As a manager, the better you know your team and what drives them, the better you can tailor your stories to match their thinking and thus the greater your influence.

Focusing on imperatives through stories

To highlight to your team what is really important, the team must be able to identify emotionally with the story, so they feel compelled to act. For example, you could describe the health and safety rules at work as written in your health and safety policy and they will leave your team cold. You could instead describe a terrible accident that befell someone who did not pay attention to the rules.

Instead of 'Rule 14 states that all production line workers must tie back long hair and wear protective headgear', tell your team that in a recent tragic accident, a staff member at your nearest competitor failed to tie back her hair and wear the headgear provided while working on an identical machine to yours. She leaned forward, her hair became trapped in the machine and she was scalped. She died in hospital the same day. Rule 14 saves lives.

Managing conflict

In times of conflict, direct action may cause more problems than it solves. Encourage each party in the conflict to tell their story: let each party in turn and without interruption explain the roots of the conflict from their perspective, their feelings, their interests and desires for resolution. The rules are simply that they must be allowed to speak uninterrupted and they must not attack the other parties involved through their story. Often the stories reveal underlying concerns of which the other parties may be unaware; they show a human side to the issue and they encourage each party to understand how it might feel to be in the others' shoes.

Outlining a vision or strategy

Imagine the CEO of a major company outlining her vision to the staff:

> Two years from now we will have increased our margins by 7 per cent, reduced our costs by 3.5 per cent, and we will begin to see a steady rise in profitability by the third quarter. Headcount is relatively static, with a freezing of a small number of posts which offset a small rise in churn . . .

This is the typical vision statement from the CEO. It's dry and boring, the figures are heard and then forgotten, and the delivery is singularly dull.

Now imagine this:

> When I was nine years old, I showed a little flair for cross-country running and would regularly be entered into local and, later, national school championships. I was a slow starter in my first races and would be overwhelmed when I saw 20 runners ahead of me. I couldn't see how I could possibly win a race with so many people to overtake. My father gave me a simple piece of advice, which has stayed with me. He said, 'You only ever have to focus on the one person in front

of you. Just overtake that one person.' Suddenly, something which had seemed overwhelming became manageable. I only had to run a little faster to overtake one person ahead of me. Then I could focus on the next, single person ahead of me.

When I joined this company I looked at our competitors and at first thought there were too many of them ahead of us for us to be considered a major competitor in this field, and then I remembered my father's advice. What was XYZ Corporation doing right now that we couldn't do better? We focused simply on being a step ahead of them. Now we found ABC ahead of us – what did we have to do to get a little ahead of them? And we have done it – working together, we have taken just a few small steps past each of our competitors and in two years have moved from twentieth in the race to third. In two years we can win this race . . .

The metaphor stays in the mind, it excites the audience and draws them into the world of the storyteller. The CEO shows her staff the possibilities through story. The figures are almost immaterial.

Final analysis

Storytelling is fun. Give yourself permission to have fun at work and start to amass a bank of stories that you can use to engage your staff, your bosses, your customers and your peers. Use personal stories, adapt others people's stories, remind yourself of incidents in your own and others' lives, think of things that have gone extraordinarily well and badly, consider times when you had successes and made mistakes. Weave a narrative through a business story and watch the effects on others.

References

Denning, S. (2011) *The Leader's Guide to Storytelling: Mastering the art and discipline of business narrative,* revised edition. San Francisco, CA: John Wiley & Sons.

Dietz, K. and Silverman, L.L. (2014) *Business Storytelling for Dummies.* Hoboken, NJ: John Wiley & Sons.

Simmons, A. (2007) *Whoever Tells the Best Story Wins: How to use your own stories to communicate with power and impact.* New York: AMACOM.

Smith, P. (2012) *Lead with a Story: A guide to crafting business narratives that captivate, convince, and inspire.* New York: AMACOM.

VAK (visual, auditory, kinaesthetic)

42

The big picture

The VAK tool will help you to understand the senses that you and others use in processing thoughts. Knowing this allows you to talk to others in a way that maps to their subconscious thinking processes, creating rapport and showing them that you truly understand them.

We do not think in words, but use words as a filter or channel to express our thoughts. (Logically, if we thought in words, we would all speak the same language.) We take in information through our five basic senses – seeing, hearing, feeling, smelling and tasting – and we process those sensory inputs internally before using words to describe them to others.

From around the age of seven, the senses of smell and taste become less important to us. For the new-born mammal with closed eyes or a limited focal length at birth, smell and taste are survival senses – we need to smell and taste our mother's milk. As we become more social animals, the senses of sight, hearing and feeling assume more importance.

If you know which primary sense someone is using as they talk to you, you can mirror this to them and so communicate at a more profound level than if you simply use your own preferred style of communication, which may mismatch theirs.

When to use it

Be aware of the differences between your own and others' VAK preferences in every conversation, no matter how formal or informal. Consider it, too, when choosing the best methods to learn something new.

How to use it

For the purposes of this explanation, people are referred to as visual, auditory and kinaesthetic. In reality, we use all the senses, but the labels are used here to distinguish between preferred/predominant styles of communication.

Visual people see internal pictures of what you say to them and of what they are about to say to you. Of course, we all see internal images, but the predominantly visual person has a greater facility to create and change these imagined images. As the visual person thinks about what they are going to say, they form an image and describe it. Because images appear and disappear at great speed, typically the visual person speaks faster than the auditory or kinaesthetic person in order to keep up with the rapid flow of pictures.

If you speak quickly, you don't have time to breathe deeply and the visual person may often appear to breathe quickly and shallowly in the upper part of the chest. If you are speaking rapidly, it may be difficult to find the words quickly; visual people often supplement what they are saying with expansive hand and arm gestures, effectively drawing pictures in the air as they speak. They use many visual terms in their speech, such as 'I see what you are saying', 'That looks clear to me', 'Can you picture this?'

Visual people learn best through pictures, diagrams, handouts, films and other visual media.

To communicate with a visual person:

- Speak relatively quickly.

- If you see the visual person gesturing with their hands and arms, gesture in exactly the same place as you respond to them. Gesturing in a different physical location or making dismissive gestures with your hands sends a signal that you don't understand the other person.

- Take pen and paper into a meeting with a visual person. Leave the paper on the table between you and, typically, they will pick it up and use it to illustrate what they are saying. They tend to become more articulate at the point at which they start to draw. A flipchart may also be useful.

- Use visual terminology in your conversation. Imagine that you are appraising a visual team member. Asking 'How do you feel about the last six months?' will be vastly less effective than 'How did you see yourself working over the last six months?' Even more usefully, if you are considering the next appraisal period, draw a line on paper, with markers indicating each month of the appraisal period, and ask the team member what they see themselves achieving at each stage.

- Notice whether their eyes defocus as you are talking to them – it is likely that they have not understood you.

Auditory (hearing) people tend to speak slower than visual people, often with a flow or musicality to their speech. They use few verbal 'tics' ('er', 'um', 'you know') and enjoy word play and creative use of language. They will often look towards the ear in which they imagine they are hearing the words that they are about to utter and sometimes gesture towards an ear. They tend to be good at remembering past conversations (often verbatim). Conversations have a structure, however loose, and the auditory person tends to be good at remembering other structures, e.g. intellectual processes and dates. They use many auditory terms in their speech, such as 'I hear what you are saying', 'That sounds good to me', 'That rings a bell'.

Auditory people learn best through lectures, conversation and debate.

To communicate with an auditory person:

- Speak at moderate speed, avoiding any verbal tics. (Every language has its own. For example, English tics include 'er', 'um', 'like', 'so', 'you know'; Swiss Germans use *genau;* Arabic speakers use *yanni.*)

- Use lots of modulation and inflection in your speech; make it musical and flowing.

- Be creative in your use of language.

- Allow them to paraphrase what you have said to check their understanding.

- Read sections of documents aloud before discussing them, rather than asking the auditory person to read them in silence.

- Try to ensure that there are no auditory distractions when you are talking to the auditory person – for example, loud conversations nearby or background music can be very distracting to them.

- Use metaphors and analogies to explain new ideas – they enjoy a good story!

Kinaesthetic (feeling) people tend to speak slower than either the visual or the auditory person. They take their time to reflect on a question before answering and may sometimes start a sentence and not finish it. They like to have physical contact either with themselves (folded arms, crossed legs, a hand on the knee as they cross their legs) or with you (touching you as they speak to you) or with inanimate objects (a pen, a TV remote control or whatever is to hand). They speak in terms of their feelings and senses: 'I have a good feeling about this', 'I don't get a sense of what you are saying', 'Hold on to that idea', 'You have to take the rough with the smooth'.

Kinaesthetic people learn best through hands-on activities, doing things that involve physical activity.

To communicate with a kinaesthetic person:

- Talk relatively slowly.

- Talk in very practical terms.

- Focus on solutions rather than problems.

- Give them time to reflect before answering and don't interrupt them.

- Take time to discuss practicalities rather than abstract concepts.

- Use feeling expressions. For example, in an appraisal, ask 'What's your feeling about the last six months?' or 'What's your sense of what you will be doing over the next six months?'

Consider, too, that when you or a team are trying to learn something new, it can be helpful to map the learning methods to your/their preferred style of thinking. The table gives some ideas:

Style	Appropriate learning methods
Visual	Mind maps
	Note making
	Slides
	Charts and tables
	YouTube clips
Auditory	Lectures
	Discussions
	Recorded learning (CDs, etc.)
	YouTube clips
	Television programmes
Kinaesthetic	Note making
	Recopying of notes
	Business games
	Taking things apart and rebuilding them
	Field trips

Final analysis

Good communicators are flexible, able to adapt their style to the people they are with. Rather than expect someone to adapt to your preferred style, sharpen your awareness, notice the predominant characteristics of someone else's style and mirror it through words, voice tone and tempo and gesture. It will have a profound effect on your ability to very quickly develop rapport and trust with others, sending out signals which suggest you really understand the other person. Like everything of worth, it takes practice to notice and mirror other people's communication styles. The rewards are worth the effort.

References

O'Connor, J. and Seymour, J. (2003) *Introducing NLP: Neuro-Linguistic Programming.* New York: Thorsons.

Ready, R. and Burton, K. (2010) *Neuro-linguistic Programming for Dummies.* Chichester, UK: John Wiley & Sons.

[PART FIFTEEN]

Conflict management

Conflict is an inevitable feature of working life. Sometimes you may find yourself in conflict with others and sometimes you may, as a manager, have to mediate when others are in conflict. At one level, conflict can be healthy. It brings issues to the surface and, if properly resolved, clears the air. But differences that simmer under the surface and occasionally flare can be hugely damaging to productive work, so the better equipped you are to deal with conflict (ideally before it escalates), the more credibility you will have as a manager.

Betari box

43

The big picture

It is uncertain who or what Betari was, but the Betari box (also known as Betari's box) has become a classic model in conflict management. The box helps you to understand the impact of your behaviour and attitudes on the behaviour and attitudes of others and shows how quickly we can descend into spirals of negative communication (see Figure 43.1).

If I feel negative about you, I will display negative behaviour towards you; this in turn will change the way you feel, resulting in negative behaviour towards me. Equally, a positive attitude from you or me can create a virtuous circle.

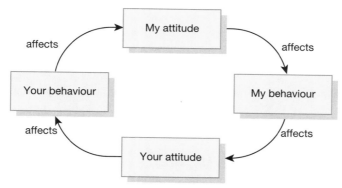

Figure 43.1 Betari box

When to use it

You can use the Betari box to remind yourself to change your patterns of behaviour if you find yourself acting negatively towards others. Equally, you can use it as a mediation tool in helping others to resolve conflict.

How to use it

If you have a team member whose negative attitude is causing problems for others, sketch out the Betari box and explain it to that team member. Often, those who create disharmony in a team are oblivious to the effects of their behaviour. Ask them to describe the feelings that trigger their behaviour and the reactions they get from others when they display that behaviour. Help them to step back from their emotional involvement in the situations that trigger their behaviour to understand how their attitudes affect what they do and how what they do has an effect on others.

If you find yourself being overly critical of a team member, step back and examine what started the negative cycle. Find a way to apologise to the team member, or make it clear that you value their contribution and, in so doing, try to start a positive cycle to counter the negative one. Learn to build on positive cycles and realise when you may be creating and building on negative cycles.

Remember that, as a manager, you are a role model for others. How you behave effectively gives permission for your team members to behave the same way. By establishing a positive cycle of behaviour with each team member, you set a great example for others to follow. You can choose how you behave towards other people, even if at some level you feel negative towards them. Choosing to maintain courteous and professional behaviour will benefit the entire team.

Final analysis

The Betari box works well because of its simplicity. It is easy to understand and explain and so provides a useful tool in helping others resolve their conflict. It's also a useful wake-up call to you when you allow negative attitudes to surface.

Reference

Beadle, P. and Murphy, J. (2013) *Why Are You Shouting at Us? The dos and don'ts of behaviour management.* London: Bloomsbury Education.

Thomas–Kilmann conflict mode instrument

44

The big picture

This classic tool is used to determine the most appropriate ways of managing conflict. Ken Thomas and Ralph Kilmann, working at the University of Pittsburgh, contended that each of us has a default mode of handling conflict (defined as situations in which the concerns of two individuals appear to be incompatible) and that our default mode may not be the best way in each situation.

The authors produced a questionnaire comprising 30 paired statements. To complete the questionnaire, users are asked to tick the single statement in each pair that is most characteristic of their behaviour and the result shows their conflict-handling preferences. Even without the questionnaire, the conflict model is extremely useful for assessing the best approach to a specific conflict situation. The model describes five possible approaches to conflict, usually shown in a two-dimensional matrix, whose vertical axis is assertiveness and horizontal axis is cooperativeness.

The terminology used in the model may not be immediately understandable. The vertical axis – assertiveness – relates to your concern for yourself or what you would take in a conflict. The horizontal axis – cooperativeness – relates to your concern for the other person in the conflict or what you would be prepared to give.

- Low assertiveness and low cooperativeness are described as 'avoiding'.

- Low assertiveness and high cooperativeness are described as 'accommodating'.

- Medium assertiveness and medium cooperativeness are described as 'compromising'.

- High assertiveness and low cooperativeness are described as 'competing'.

- High assertiveness and high cooperativeness are described as 'collaborating.'

So, for example, when you are accommodating, you are giving the other party what they want without taking anything for yourself.

When to use it

Use the model any time you find yourself involved in conflict or need to help others (for example, your team members) to resolve a conflict. You may be interested in purchasing the questionnaire to determine your preferred style, but the model alone is enough to help you to determine the most appropriate method to deal with a conflict.

How to use it

When faced with a conflict, determine how critical its resolution is to you and others. Consider to what extent you are prepared to give something to the other side and to what extent you are prepared to take from them. On that basis, the key below should help you to select the best approach:

Competing is high in assertiveness and low in cooperativeness (or all take and no give). Here you are prepared to pursue your own requirements at the expense of the other person. Use this approach when there is no question of discussion around an issue; when it is critical that you achieve your own objective; when it is not important to leave the door open to future negotiation; when the other person is simply wrong and any other stance would allow them to make a mistake that is costly for them, you or others.

Accommodating is low in assertiveness and high in cooperativeness – the very opposite of competing. You may choose to accommodate the other person out of pure self-sacrifice and it may seem a submissive stance. However, it can be used as a long-term ploy. Imagine, for example, that you have something that is perceived as being of high value to the other person but of low value to you. Give it away now and you can call in a favour from the other person later. Imagine it a little like a loss leader in a retail store – the store gives you something for nothing and because you think well of the store as a result, you may choose to shop there again and tell other people about it.

Avoiding is low in assertiveness and low in cooperativeness. You may choose to walk away from a conflict for diplomatic reasons, because it is not worth investing time in this conflict when you have bigger battles to fight later on, because it is not worth the energy it would take, because the other person has more vested interest in resolving the situation than you do.

Collaborating is both high in assertiveness and high in cooperativeness. In col-laborating, you have avoided confrontation and worked hard to understand each other's underlying interests. Often, negotiations fail because each side has a desire to 'win' and this mindset militates against collaborative problem solving and decision making. People negotiate around 'positions' ('I want a 50 per cent pay rise,' 'Well, I am not going to give you a pay rise') instead of 'interests' ('I need an increased salary because I cannot support my family at my current salary level'). Collaboration seeks to discover the underlying reasons for conflict.

Compromising is intermediate in both assertiveness and cooperativeness. Compromising gives each party just part of what they want and so creates an uneasy peace. It is a shorter step from compromising to collaborating than from avoiding or competing to collaborating and so may feel a more comfortable solution, but it may leave you feeling that you wanted more or gave away too much. Consider it a stepping stone towards complete collaboration and use it to gain trust and demonstrate positive intentions.

Final analysis

Once you understand the language of Thomas–Kilmann's conflict mode instrument, it becomes a powerful tool in your armoury. It is far better to approach conflict in the most appropriate way from the outset than to get it wrong at the beginning and have to backtrack. Study each approach and consider how you have resolved or failed to resolve a conflict in the past. Which method did you adopt? Where the conflict was not readily resolved, would one of the other approaches have been more appropriate? As you learn from your experience, so the application of the model will become quite intuitive.

References

Lencioni, P.M. (2005) *Overcoming the Five Dysfunctions of a Team: A field guide for leaders, managers, and facilitators.* San Francisco, CA: John Wiley & Sons.

Thomas, K.W. (2002) *Thomas–Kilmann conflict mode instrument.* Mountain View, CA: CPP, Inc.

PART SIXTEEN

Creativity

Creativity is largely unmanageable. Spontaneity can't easily be channelled and creative people can be viewed as non-conformists or mavericks in a rigidly structured or regulated workplace. Everyone is capable of being creative, given the right tools, time and encouragement, so while we can't manage creativity, we can create an environment that allows it to flourish.

Of the many creative thinking tools extant, this small collection includes models which can be used in the moment, without special equipment, and with the potential to create startling results. Give 'permission' for your team members to think creatively!

45

Brain-friendly brainstorming

The big picture

In traditional brainstorming, a problem is declared, interested parties call out possible solutions, a scribe writes them down and later the ideas are evaluated. It's a long-used, tried-and-tested model and within limits, it works. Consider, though, some of the brainstorming sessions in which you have taken part. They have two major flaws – first, you could probably have listed most of the ideas yourself because they are fairly pedestrian, obvious and lacking in creativity, and second, the most senior person or the one with the loudest voice will tend to dominate the evaluation phase and defend their ideas, whether or not they merited such a spirited defence.

Brain-friendly brainstorming solves both these problems, and very simply. It allows the group to be more creative in a shorter space of time and democratically filter out the ideas that are not worth further discussion.

When to use it

Brainstorming is useful whenever you need a broad range of possible solutions to a shared problem.

How to use it

Have you ever had the experience of struggling to find a solution to a problem and finally walking away from it? As you relax or think of something unrelated to the problem, the solution suddenly emerges. While the 'Eureka!' moment may feel magical, in reality, the moment you step away from a burning problem, your sub-conscious continues to work on it, looking back through your experiences, finding similar (resolved) issues and then presenting the solution to you without giving you the rationale behind it. Intuition is nothing more than unconscious experience.

Brain-friendly brainstorming works on the same principles: if you continue to work on a problem, the subconscious has little chance to relate it to experiences and the critical faculty of the conscious mind intervenes. In brain-friendly brainstorming, you simply need to introduce a break in which you and other participants discuss something unrelated to the current problem. As you resume the brainstorming, you'll find lots of creative solutions emerging.

The method is:

1 State the problem, ensuring that everyone understands the issue and any contextual information that may help in their thinking.

2 Appoint a scribe, ideally using a flipchart or whiteboard, so that everything written is immediately visible to participants (because one idea may spawn another).

3 Brainstorm for two minutes, then stop.

4 Introduce another topic of conversation that has no relationship to the original problem and talk to each other for another two minutes.

5 Resume the brainstorming and call out ideas for a further two minutes.

At this stage, you will have a long list of ideas, with most of the creative solutions appearing in the second session. To assess quickly which ideas are worthy of further consideration:

1 Use three pens – one red, one green and one neutral (black or blue).

2 The scribe should call out each item on the brainstormed list, checking where necessary that everyone understands the item (but avoiding discussion or justifications from the participants).

3 The scribe asks for a show of hands:

(a) Who thinks the idea has merit and is worth further discussion?

(b) Who thinks the idea is not worth further discussion?

(c) Who thinks the idea may be interesting to discuss at another time but is not strictly relevant to this problem?

4 If the majority believe the idea has merit, mark it with a green plus sign; if the majority believe the idea has no merit, mark it with a red minus sign; if the majority now believe that the idea is simply interesting, mark it with a black or blue 'i'.

In this way, you will have a filtered list of creative solutions in less than ten minutes.

Final analysis

We have a tendency to hold on to old techniques because they are familiar and believed to be effective. Armed with better knowledge of how the brain works, it's useful to try new methods which can result in more effective solutions, quicker. Brain-friendly brainstorming is deceptively simple – the start, stop, start produces creative answers and the plus/minus/interesting gives you a worthwhile list in almost no time. Now you can spend more time on establishing how the creative and approved ideas can be put into practice.

Reference

Curedale, R.A. (2013) *50 Brainstorming Methods: For team and individual ideation.* Topanga, CA: Design Community College Inc.

Challenging assumptions

46

The big picture

Challenging assumptions is a simple and hugely powerful creative tool based on the notion that nothing is real – we have simply assumed it to be so.

When to use it

Challenging assumptions can be used for redesign of processes, systems and machines.

How to use it

Imagine that you have long used a specific process at work. Nobody has questioned its efficacy since it was first implemented, but you are aware that time has moved on and there may be a more effective approach. Working in a small group or alone, simply list all the elements or steps in the current process. These are the current 'truths' – they are all we know about the current process.

Now take each element or step in turn and tell yourself or the group that this is not a fact, it is not real, it is just an assumption. We have assumed that it is the right step in the right place. What would happen if we removed it, or changed it, or perhaps substituted something else for it? Very quickly, you'll find redundant steps, steps out of sequence, steps that no longer have any validity.

To illustrate the idea, think back a few decades to a time when telephones were heavy devices that sat on a desktop. At that time, that's all we knew about telephones. List everything you knew, treat it as an assumption and then see how you could change, modernise, adapt or eliminate it (see the table).

Assumptions about a telephone	What we could do instead
It has wires.	Make it wireless.
It has a separate base and handset.	Make them one unit.
We call people by dialling their numbers.	Use push buttons, voice control or a keypad.
It has a ringtone.	Use music.
It is heavy and cannot be moved.	Make it portable.

As you'll see, in just a few minutes you've invented the first mobile telephone. When mobile phones appeared, most of the technologies required to make them had existed for a long time (wireless telegraphy dates from the 1870s) but nobody had thought to combine them. By challenging assumptions, you can become very inventive very quickly.

Final analysis

Challenging assumptions is a quick and elegant way of rationalising processes, systems and machines, of being innovative without requiring the brain of an inventor. It is more fun to use as a collaborative problem-solving or generative tool. Use it with your team members to develop their inventiveness and playfulness.

References

De Bono, E. (2009) *Lateral Thinking: A textbook of creativity.* New York: Penguin.

Morgan, A. and Barden, M. (2015) *A Beautiful Constraint: How to transform your limitations into advantages, and why it's everyone's business.* Hoboken, NJ: John Wiley & Sons.

PMI (plus, minus, interesting)

47

The big picture

We have already encountered PMI as a filtering tool for brain-friendly brainstorming, but PMI can be used as a creative tool in its own right. Using PMI you can create something new from even the silliest sounding ideas. The concept comes from Edward de Bono, a leading light in the world of creative thinking.

When to use it

Use PMI to generate new ideas or to explore what may otherwise be cast off as silly or impractical ideas. It's important that you, as a manager, encourage creative thinking in your team. If someone at a team meeting suggests something that others reject, it can be discouraging for the team member who later may not contribute to a meeting for fear of looking foolish. Rather than agreeing with the group and rejecting the idea, use PMI as a way of exploring whether there is the germ of a solution somewhere inside that idea.

How to use it

1 Take the idea or statement and for one minute brainstorm only the positives.

2 Now brainstorm the negatives for one minute.

3 Finally, ask: what was interesting about this?

Note that you could combine this with brain-friendly brainstorming and spend one minute on, one minute off and one minute on each step.

You'll be surprised at the positive ideas that are spawned by the first idea, and focusing only on positives gives licence to those participating to be playful and silly. Even if the original idea is rejected, the PMI process may generate useful new ideas, which you can put into practice.

Final analysis

Creative thinking is all about unexpected connections and PMI is a useful way of triggering those connections. Separating the discussion into pluses, minuses and interesting ideas ensures that you do not get bogged down in debate or endless justifications of an idea – instead, you create a relaxed atmosphere in which the ideas simply flow.

Reference

De Bono, E. (2006) *De Bono's Thinking Course: Powerful tools to transform your thinking.* London: BBC Active.

Random word technique

48

The big picture

Random word technique is a tool to enable you to generate creative ideas to resolve difficult problems. To be creative you need to think beyond the obvious. If we have a problem to solve, we may bring with us a lot of baggage related to the problem. Because we know something of the nature of the problem, we tend to solve it within the confines of that knowledge. Random word technique allows you to throw off the shackles of existing knowledge, take the problem to a different level, then return to the original problem with fresh, new ideas.

When to use it

Any time you need a range of solutions to a problem, the random word technique may help.

How to use it

1 When faced with a problem, choose a page and a line randomly from a book that is not related to the problem area.

2 Take the first noun or descriptive word on the chosen line.

3 Freely list anything you associate with the object that the noun describes.

4 Now apply those ideas to the original problem area.

Here's an example to illustrate the method:

A restaurateur is struggling to fill his restaurant. The food is excellent, the service standards are high, but the location is poor. Few people naturally pass the restaurant, which is on a side street just off a main shopping street in a big city. The public is tantalisingly close but cannot see the restaurant from the main road.

The restaurateur needs to get more people into the restaurant. He calls together his staff. They choose a book, randomly, call out a page and line number and the first noun on that line is *hammer*. They call out and write down everything they associate with a hammer, no matter how tenuous the link, then associate some of the ideas back to the original problem of getting more people in the restaurant (see the table).

Ideas called out	Related back to the original problem
Metal	Combine heavy and metal (below): have music-themed nights with live bands to attract different audiences – a heavy metal night, jazz night, cocktail pianist.
Heavy	(As above.)
Repeat action	Give loyalty vouchers offering discount for return visits.
Wood	Get someone to wear an advertising sign on their back on the main shopping street, with a wooden hand pointing to the restaurant. Re-theme the restaurant as an oak-panelled, old-fashioned ladies' or gentlemen's club, and have alternate ladies' and gentlemen's evenings/lunches.
DIY (do it yourself)	Allow children to decorate their own pizza bases, which we cook.
Noisy	Have a disco after the last meal has been served. Have a silent disco (dancers wear headphones, so neighbours are not disturbed). Invite local societies and clubs to hold their meetings here, offering discount for volume bookings as a society takes over the restaurant for a lunchtime or evening.
Nails	Bring in a beautician once a week who offers therapies before lunch.
Create	Create sandwiches and lunch boxes for local business people. Deliver to their offices.

From such a simple idea, a whole list of creative ideas emerges.

Final analysis

Random word technique is one of the most powerful creative thinking techniques, because it releases you from the relatively narrow confines of your existing knowledge of your business area. Again it allows playfulness in the thinking – nothing is ever rejected and participants start to make extraordinary connections and associations. It's also a great team-bonding exercise.

Reference

De Bono, E. (2009) *Lateral Thinking: A textbook of creativity.* New York: Penguin.

49 SCAMPER

The big picture

We often do things at work in a particular way because we have always done it that way. Sometimes it is useful to step back and re-examine our standard processes and systems to see whether we can find ways to improve them.

SCAMPER was devised in the 1970s by Robert Eberle, an educational administrator from Illinois, to help children to become more creative. He built on the work of Alex Osborn (1888–1996), who was credited with the invention of brainstorming. Osborn, who worked in advertising, had compiled with his staff a list of 83 questions designed to spark creative thinking. Eberle simplified the list and created the acronym SCAMPER as an easy-to-recall mnemonic.

SCAMPER stands for:

- **S**ubstitute
- **C**ombine
- **A**dapt
- **M**odify (magnify, minify)
- **P**ut to another use
- **E**liminate
- **R**everse (rearrange)

When to use it

You can use SCAMPER either to generate new ideas or to improve upon existing ideas, systems, equipment, processes or controls.

How to use it

Select, for example, a product that your organisation is marketing and try some of the following:

Substitute	Substitute one part of the product for another. Substitute something new for an existing part of the product.
Combine	Combine two elements of the product. Combine the product with another product.
Adapt	Adapt the product to be used in different ways. Adapt part of the product to operate differently within the product itself or in a different product or context altogether.
Modify (magnify, minify)	Change part of the product. Make the product or part of it smaller. Make the product or part of it bigger.
Put to another use	Use the product in a new or different context. Market it to a different target group, different age range, geographical market.
Eliminate	Take out a part of the product – does it now work more effectively? Have you created something new as a result?
Reverse (rearrange)	Either reverse some elements of the product or rearrange them to work differently or more efficiently.

Final analysis

You don't have to try everything here, SCAMPER simply provides a checklist of possibilities. If an element of SCAMPER does not fit the idea that you are playing with, see how you can adapt it to prompt questions which in turn generate new ideas.

Reference

Robert Eberle's original book *SCAMPER* is now out of print, but there are many internet articles on the technique.

PART
SEVENTEEN

Giving feedback

Many managers become nervous before giving feedback, apologising for having to raise an issue with their team members and diluting the feedback to such an extent that its intent is lost.

It was traditional to offer feedback in a 'sandwich' – say something positive (first slice of bread), slip in the real feedback (the filling) and quickly add another positive (second slice of bread), then sigh with relief that it was over. The method never worked because it obscured the real point of the feedback. Imagine:

You did a great job this morning, your work standards in general are not up to our expectations, but you did a really good job this morning.

What's the message here?

Think of feedback simply as information rather than as positive or negative. The recipient can choose to do something with that information, not do something with it or hold on to it for later use.

It is important that feedback describes behaviour and does not attack the person. Separate the two in your mind before you deliver the feedback or you may be accused of bullying or aggression.

Having a framework for delivering feedback should increase your confidence that you are giving a clear message in a useful sequence. In this section there are two feedback frameworks: the first, EEC, is used for relatively minor, everyday feedback, either to encourage good behaviour or to discourage bad; the second, EENC, is designed for feedback on more serious issues.

Be careful to give feedback as quickly as possible when you see aberrant behaviour. If you leave it too long, you forfeit the right to give any feedback. Imagine telling a team member that you have noticed they have never attended a team meeting in the five years since they joined the team. They have every right to question why you did not raise the issue five years ago if you considered it to be important. If you defer giving feedback, there is a danger that it assumes a greater importance in your mind and so, by the time you do deliver it, you risk implying that it is much more serious than it is in reality.

Document your feedback discussions. If an issue escalates to the point at which it becomes central to disciplinary proceedings, you will need to provide documentary evidence that you had discussed the issue with your team member. The single biggest reason for the failure of disciplinary proceedings is the lack of documentary evidence from the manager and then you are reliant on hearsay – your claims to have raised an issue with a team member may be met with their claims that you did not.

50

EEC model

The big picture

Very often people are oblivious to the effects that their behaviour is having on others. Good feedback should make it clear that the behaviour is not acceptable and help the recipient choose alternative behaviour.

When to use it

The EEC model is useful both for encouraging the individual to repeat something useful or beneficial or to stop doing something that is not acceptable.
  EEC stands for:

- **E**xample
- **E**ffects
- **C**ontinue/**C**hange

How to use it

Let's see how to use it to reinforce positive behaviour:

I understand that George was late arriving at work yesterday and that you very kindly took his calls until he arrived [**E**xample]. *Had you not picked up the call from ABC Corporation and handled it so calmly and positively, it could have soured our relationship with them. I heard later from Tessa at ABC that you were very helpful, able to give her the information she needed and she was delighted* [**E**ffects]. *George is likely to be late for the next two mornings, because of another* *project he is working on. If you could field his calls again for the next two mornings until he is back to a normal working pattern, that would be really helpful. Thank you [**C**ontinue].*

Let's now see the same structure used for feedback on undesirable behaviour. Here the style of delivery is a little different. When reinforcing positive behaviour it is reasonable to offer it as a monologue. In challenging aberrant behaviour, it is important to ask the recipient to offer a solution so that they, rather than you, 'own' that solution.

*It is really important that our two new team members feel that they can contribute usefully in team discussions. I have noticed at the last couple of team meetings, you have interrupted them and talked over them each time they have tried to join in the discussions [**E**xample] and, seeing how dejected they look each time this happens, I have a real concern that they will stop trying to say anything if you continue to do this [**E**ffects]. How can you help to make it easier for them to join in and feel more valued members of the team [**C**hange]?*

Final analysis

EEC offers a neat structure for giving feedback, whether or not you use it to encourage positive behaviour or to eliminate unacceptable behaviour. Be careful to use each element of the model in sequence – it is far more powerful to give an example first, then discuss the effects and finally the next steps. Be careful not to apologise for giving feedback and avoid any other discussions before or after it that weaken the feedback.

Reference

There are no known books that relate specifically to the EEC model, but many online resources offer both this version and variants of the model.

51 EENC

The big picture

The EEC model is useful for simple, straightforward feedback. EENC is designed for more serious issues, when it is important that the team member be in no doubt that the issue is serious and that there will be consequences if the behaviour continues.
EENC stands for:

- **E**xample: what you have observed; be precise.
- **E**motion: how you, as manager, feel about it; state your feelings but do not display them.
- **N**eeds: what the team member needs to do about it.
- **C**onsequences: what will happen if they do or do not change their behaviour.

When to use it

Use EENC when you consider that if the team member continues to behave in an unacceptable way, you may have to resolve the problem through disciplinary proceedings or using other formal mechanisms.

How to use it

In reality, you would discuss the behaviour with your team member and EENC would be used as a structure for that discussion. First let's see how each component works in an example given as a monologue, then let's see how this might work in practice as a dialogue with the team member:

I've noticed that over the last week you have arrived between 30 and 60 minutes late every morning, despite our discussions last month about the importance of *arriving on time so that your team members do not have to keep covering for you in your absence [**E**xample]. I am disappointed that, despite our recent discussion, you continue to arrive late [**E**motion]. I need to see you arriving on time in future, and if there is any chance that you will not, I need you to inform me beforehand so that we can arrange cover for you without distracting others from their work [**N**eeds]. If you do, I am prepared to overlook it this time. If you do not, you know that I will have to take this issue to a more formal level [**C**onsequences]. I will send you an email documenting this conversation and I would like you to send back an email acknowledging it. Thank you.*

In practice, you should be addressing a *change* in behaviour rather than a long-standing behavioural issue and the team member must have the right of reply:

*I've noticed that over the last week you have arrived between 30 and 60 minutes late every morning, despite our discussions last month about the importance of arriving on time so that your team members do not have to keep covering for you in your absence. You were always an excellent timekeeper in the past. What has changed [**E**xample]?*

It may be that the team member had a valid reason for arriving late and simply hadn't discussed it with you. It may be that the team member *had* told you and you had forgotten. It's important that you allow them the right of reply before moving on to the next part of the feedback.

*I am disappointed that, despite our recent discussion, you continue to arrive late [**E**motion].*

Be careful to choose the appropriate emotion here and not to display that emotion. Shouting at the team member that you are angry is both unhelpful and unprofessional. Quietly stating that you are angry is much more powerful than an overt display of anger. Choose carefully the word you use to describe your feelings about your team member's behaviour. 'Disappointed' is the type of word used by parents and teachers to their children. While it can make the person feel ashamed of their behaviour, it might also be construed as patronising. The idea here is to show the recipient of your feedback that this is serious and that you are taking it personally.

*What are you going to do differently [**N**eeds]?*

If you ask the recipient to tell you what they will do differently they are more likely to 'own' the solution and do something about it.

Now you have a choice. You can either tell them the consequences of action or inaction (as in the monologue example above) or you can ask them to tell you:

*Put yourself in my shoes for a moment. If I were reporting to you and I consistently arrived late, how would you deal with it [**C**onsequences]?*

Very often you will find that the team member designs a far worse outcome than you had planned. At this point, you can appear the liberal manager and suggest that, while this may be a little heavy-handed on this occasion, you know that, should the behaviour continue, you will have to take things to a more formal level.

Again, document the discussion in an email and request an email acknowledgement, so that you have the necessary evidence should the matter escalate.

Final analysis

The EENC model is a powerful tool and should be used only when you are certain of your ground, you can give specific examples of the aberrant behaviour and you are prepared to take further action if the behaviour does not improve. In most cases, you will find that you only have to use this structure once and the team member will understand immediately that this is serious and will be unlikely to 'reoffend'.

Reference

There are no known books that relate specifically to the EENC model, but many online resources offer both this version and variants of the model.

[PART EIGHTEEN]

Goal setting

There is a story that only 3 per cent of students leaving Yale University in a particular year wrote their goals in the yearbook. Twenty years later, their net worth was greater than that of the other 97 per cent put together. The story is apocryphal and denied by the university. It does, however, illustrate the thinking prevalent in organisations that everyone will be more successful if they set goals.

There is a danger in goal setting that you sell yourself short. You set a goal that is highly achievable and you meet it. You don't learn from it, you didn't stretch yourself and you may well have achieved without formalising the goal in the first place. The debate continues and the jury is still out, determining whether continual improvement is better than major goal setting.

For now, most of our organisations will encourage us to set goals, and it's useful to have a framework for constructing them which may increase our chances of achieving them.

Locke and Latham's five principles

52

The big picture

Professors Edwin Locke (Maryland University) and Gary Latham (University of Toronto) believed that there are five basic principles for setting goals and that the likelihood of achievement increases according to the level of adherence to each of the principles. They are:

- Clarity
- Challenge
- Commitment
- Feedback
- Task complexity

When to use it

The five principles can be applied whenever you are working with a team member to set new goals.

How to use it

- **Clarity**: state a goal clearly, concisely and unambiguously. Specify a time period in which the team member must achieve the goal. Ensure that the outcome can be measured in some way. Test the team member's understanding of the goal. Asking the team member to tell you what you just said merely tests memory but not understanding. If the team member can paraphrase the goal, and even start to explain the first steps towards achieving it, then it is likely that he has understood the goal.

- **Challenge**: a goal must be challenging, encouraging a sense of motivation to attain the goal and a sense of achievement when it is fulfilled. The difficulty here may be balancing challenge with a realistic view of what your team member can truly achieve. Too difficult, and the team member will be demotivated; too easy and there will be no sense of achievement. The extent of the challenge will have a direct relationship to the amount of time you will need to devote to monitoring the team member's progress and the level of intervention you may be required to give.

- **Commitment**: people tend to work better when they feel they own an assignment or task. Help the team member to feel a sense of ownership of the goal and help them to see how it aligns with strategic or operational goals, so that they see the relevance of their achievements within the context of the broader team or organisation. Remove any obstacles to their achievement so that as much as possible is within their control.

- **Feedback**: establish at the outset how you will give feedback, and encourage the team member to assess their own progress. How often will you meet? How should the team member report to you? How detailed should those reports be? Will you be available to help?

- **Task complexity**: if a goal is too complex, the team member will struggle to achieve it and become demotivated. It is important that you remove any barriers and give the individual sufficient time to achieve the goal and help them to learn from the experience.

Final analysis

The five principles offer a common-sense and practical framework for goal setting. Where SMART (see Chapter 54) principles give a structure for the goal itself, the five principles offer useful guidance to the management of goal setting.

Reference

The model first appeared in:

Locke, E.A. and Latham, G.P. (1989) *A Theory of Goal Setting and Performance.* Harlow, UK: Prentice Hall.

It is now out of print and copies are exchanged at vastly more than the original cover price. There are many articles on the internet which describe the model in detail.

Reticular activating system

53

The big picture

Knowledge of the way that the brain helps us focus and drives out 'noise' is useful in helping us to focus on the things that we want, without missing out on vital things that could help us attain our goals. The reticular activating system (RAS) is a filtering system, which filters into our conscious awareness those things that are relevant to what we are particularly interested in and filters out any extraneous information. In physiological terms, the RAS is responsible for the transitions between a relaxed waking state and periods of high attention.

Imagine that you are about to buy a new car. You assess various models before deciding upon the one you want to purchase. You look out into the street and it seems to be filled with exactly the make and model of car you want, possibly even in the same colour. After some deliberation, you change your mind and decide on another model. The original model seems to have disappeared from the streets to be replaced by the new model. Of course, each model was there before you became interested in it, but the RAS filters out other models because you are focusing so intently on your chosen model.

Imagine that you develop a new interest, which becomes an all-consuming passion. Suddenly you begin to notice radio broadcasts, television programmes, books and magazine articles devoted to your new interest. You start to meet people who have experience of the very thing that is obsessing you. The RAS has refocused your attention to filter everything relevant to your newfound passion.

There is an old Buddhist saying: 'When the pupil is ready, the teacher will appear.' In reality, the teacher was always there, but you didn't need her until you became interested in her subject.

The RAS is particularly useful in goal setting. If you can create clear goals for yourself, the RAS will help you to find all the resources you need to achieve them.

When to use it

Be aware of the RAS whenever you are setting goals for yourself and others.

How to use it

You can effectively program the RAS to help a team member to achieve a goal. Ask your team member to visualise exactly what it would feel like to have achieved the goal. What would they be seeing that they are not seeing now? What would they be hearing that is different from now? For example, a team member striving for a specific promotion might imagine a feeling of immense pride, hearing praise from others and seeing the team from a different perspective as they look out from their new office.

By engaging as many senses as possible in goal setting, the team member will start to think about the goal as though it has already been achieved – they are starting to live it now. The RAS then focuses on all the things they need to do now to achieve the goal. It does not distinguish between reality and imagined events and so the clearer the image of the goal in the team member's mind, the more effectively the RAS will work to help the team member to focus on precisely what needs to happen to attain the goal. Help the team member to develop some positive affirmations (see Chapter 1) to reinforce the work of the RAS.

Final analysis

Just as a knowledge of the RAS will help you in goal setting for your team members, so you can apply it to personal goal setting. As you read this chapter you may be struck by the similarities between the RAS and the thinking behind the law of attraction (see Chapter 9). While the law of attraction has found something of a New Age cult following, the RAS provides a more practical explanation of the idea that you get what you focus on.

Reference

Baggett, B.A. (2015) *The Magic Question: How to get what you want in half the time* (Kindle edition). Available from: Amazon.com (accessed 12 May 2015).

SMART goals

54

The big picture

The SMART mnemonic has been the staple tool for goal and objective setting in businesses since the early 1980s, but is often poorly implemented and misinterpreted. Used well, it gives a solid basis for a well-formed goal or objective. One of the issues with SMART is that there is no standard interpretation for the acronym. In early versions it was translated as Specific, Measurable, Achievable, Realistic and Timebound. There is obvious redundancy in this definition – if it is achievable, then it is realistic, and vice versa. Variants include:

- Specific, stretching
- Measurable, meaningful
- Achievable, agreed
- Realistic, rewarding, relevant
- Timebound, tangible, timely

The most useful expansion of the acronym, and one that is becoming more widely adopted, is:

- **S**pecific
- **M**easurable
- **A**chievable
- **R**elevant
- **T**imebound

When to use it

SMART provides a very useful structure for objective or goal setting.

How to use it

When setting goals for team members, use SMART as a checklist to ensure that the objective is comprehensive and unambiguous. Let's look at each element in turn.

- **Specific**: what, specifically, are you asking the team member to achieve? It is important that you get this right. An appraisal is not the time to dispute the meaning of a goal set six months earlier. It needs to be absolutely clear from the outset.

- **Measurable**: how, precisely, will it be measured? If you were to pick up a bow and arrow for the first time and fire at a target, you would be delighted if the arrow struck the target at all. While you may have been aiming for the bull's-eye in the centre, you probably had no real expectation of hitting it. If you ask a team member to meet a particular target, are they expected to hit it exactly? Is there some tolerance in the measure? Can they expect to be reprimanded if they do not meet it exactly? What happens if they exceed the target? What concrete evidence can the team member provide to show that they have met the target? How will it be measured? There are only four elements that can be measured or monitored – quantity, cost, time and quality. The first three have specific measurement scales attached to them; quality is intangible and sometimes highly subjective. Your goal in making the objective specific and measurable is to set expectations absolutely clearly so that when you appraise the team member, there can be no arguments such as 'Well, I didn't know what you meant by that' or 'Oh! I interpreted that to mean . . .'

- **Achievable**: not only should the objective or goal be achievable, based on the team member's current level of skill, knowledge and experience, but it should stretch them beyond exactly what they know now and can do already so that they learn and develop as they achieve it. The team member cannot work in isolation from others in the organisation and you have a role, as their manager, in removing obstacles to the team member's achievement of their goal.

- **Relevant**: set goals that are relevant to the individual, to the team or department, and to the organisation. In the best-run organisations there is a clear cascade from strategy through business plans to objectives. Indeed, it should be possible to take a random set of objectives (discounting behavioural objectives) from across an organisation and from them piece together a high-level view of the organisation's strategy. If you cannot link an objective or goal to the organisation's strategic intent, then the goal is likely to be irrelevant. Following this logic, a team's goals must meet organisational needs and an individual's goals must meet team needs. In the ideal world, relevance to the individual also includes the need to set objectives that help the individual's personal and professional development. In reality, of course, some jobs simply have to be done, and there may be only one person available to do them.

- **Timebound**: when should the work start and finish? Are there interim deadlines to be met? Is the timing realistic given the team member's other work commitments and (particularly in a matrix structure) reporting lines?

Final analysis

SMART has stood the test of time because it encompasses everything that needs to be agreed in goal and objective setting. In high-performing teams, it is a great springboard for personal motivation and development. In tick-box cultures it is a largely meaningless exercise, poorly implemented and contributing little to personal and team development. Use it well!

Reference

Dallas, J. (2015) *Smart Goals: Everything you need to know about setting S.M.A.R.T. goals* (Kindle edition). Available from: Amazon.com (accessed 12 May 2015).

55

CASE – behavioural objectives

The big picture

The SMART mnemonic is useful for setting task-based objectives but is a poor basis for behavioural objectives. The CASE mnemonic is designed specifically for setting behavioural objectives. CASE stands for:

- **C**ontext: what, specifically, have you observed the team member doing?
- **A**ction: what action will the team member now take to remedy that behaviour?
- **S**tandards: what organisational standards are you asking the team member to uphold?
- **E**valuation: how will you agree to monitor the team member's progress against the objective?

When to use it

Use CASE whenever you need something a little more powerful than one-to-one feedback to help a team member to rectify a behavioural issue.

How to use it

First (and very importantly), give the team member direct feedback about the errant behaviour. You may consider using the EEC structure from this book (see Chapter 50). Then create the CASE objective, documenting it as you discuss it with the team member.

A CASE objective can be written in the third person: 'Over the last two months, Fred has . . .' or in the first person, as if by the team member: 'Over the last two months I have . . .' It may be easier to persuade the team member that you should document the objective in the third person so that it does not sound like a police witness statement, but there is real power in a statement in the first person.

Imagine the team member is taking too many smoking breaks during the day. Your CASE objective might read like this:

- **Context:** over the last two months, Fred has taken an average of 10 smoking breaks during standard working hours, each break taking some 7–8 minutes.

- **Action:** Fred will, henceforth, take smoking breaks during the mid-morning and mid-afternoon coffee breaks and at lunchtime.

- **Standards:** Fred's contracted hours are 9.00 to 17.00, with 15-minute breaks between 10.30 and 10.45 and 15.15 and 15.30 and a lunch break of an hour to be taken between 12.30 and 14.00.

- **Evaluation:** I will monitor Fred's absences during the working day over the next seven days and should Fred wish to take additional breaks, he must gain my agreement first.

Then sign and date the document and ask Fred to do the same. The main reason disciplinary proceedings fail is because of lack of documented evidence by the manager. Where nothing is documented, the proceedings are based largely around hearsay.

Final analysis

Before creating a CASE objective, check first with your HR department that they will support you in its use. Try not to be too draconian in the application of CASE – in most situations, simple feedback offered sufficiently early is enough to prevent unacceptable behaviour. Only where you sense resistance to change, or feel that you need to impress upon the team member the seriousness of the feedback, might you consider a documented CASE objective.

Reference

Cotton, D. (2014) *Managing Difficult People in a Week (Teach Yourself in A Week)*. London: Teach Yourself.

[PART NINETEEN]

Influence and persuasion

As a manager, you will have to persuade people to do things they don't necessarily want to do, sell ideas to bosses, peers and team members, and persuade others to support you, whether publicly or privately. Influence and persuasion are key management skills. They require an understanding of other people's motivational drivers and an ability to be flexible in your approach to others. What follow are some tremendously powerful models of influence and persuasion. Use them carefully, so you avoid treading the tightrope between influence and manipulation.

56

4Ps of persuasion

The big picture

The 4Ps are the qualities that you need to be able to persuade and influence others. The way that others perceive you affects the level of influence you will have over them. By focusing on the 4Ps you can create the best impression in other people's minds and so develop your ability to influence and persuade.

The 4Ps are:

- **P**ower
- **P**ositioning
- **P**oliteness
- **P**erformance

When to use it

Use the 4Ps as a mental checklist of the attributes you need to display in influencing others.

How to use it

Power

There are two kinds of power:

1 Internal power is the power that people perceive that you exude from the inside out. For example, self-confidence, self-esteem, charisma, physical presence, gravitas, spirituality.

2 External power is the power that others attribute to you because of, for example, your position at work, your expertise in a certain area, your power to reward or disrupt.

Assess your levels of power in each of these areas, taking care in how you use external power. For example, using your position at work to legitimise your actions can be seen as aggressive, bullying and a misuse of power. Expertise is highly valued as long as you are generous with your time in disseminating knowledge. It can be easy to hold on to information and dispense it as a favour or when you see fit. The power to reward is a double-edged sword. You can make it clear that if others perform the way you want, you will reward them, but the veiled threat is that a failure to conform to your idea of high performance may result in punishment or failure to progress. Finally, the power to disrupt casts a long shadow over any working relationships.

Internal power is more useful in influencing others as long as you don't overwork it. For example, too much confidence can be overwhelming for others. High self-esteem must be backed up by performance. Charismatic people can fill a room with their presence but need to know when to switch it off and become part of the group. Overbearing physical presence can be threatening to others. Spirituality can manifest itself as piety and alienate others.

In all of these areas, it is important that you strive for balance.

Positioning

This is the perception that others have of you and how they talk about you, whether in your presence or absence. It will be shaped by the other three Ps. Make a habit of stepping regularly into other people's shoes and imagine how you appear to them.

Politeness

Be courteous and fair. Listen to people and make them feel good about themselves. Most people like to do things for people who are nice to them. Be assertive without showing aggression.

Performance

If you are believed to be competent at what you do, you will have greater influence over others.

Final analysis

The 4Ps provide a useful wake-up call to consider others and further develop your self-awareness. Perception is reality and whatever you believe you are displaying to others, ultimately it is only their perceptions that count. Be prepared to accept other people's feedback graciously, consider it and change your behaviour accordingly.

When something that you are doing is not working, don't persist doggedly in the hope that you will elicit a different reaction from others. If it isn't working then change it. The old adage 'If you always do what you always did, you'll always get what you always got' can be extended to '. . . so if you want to get something different, do something different or you deserve what you get'.

People are more easily persuaded by people they like and trust. If they can see something of themselves in you, or a quality in you that they would like to emulate, persuasion becomes far easier. It is not enough to expect that people will listen to you and follow you simply because you occupy a managerial position. Leaders have followers and leaders are not leaders because of a title, but because they do or say something that inspires others to listen and follow them. As a manager, don't expect that your position alone sells ideas. Consider others, the impression you are creating, and look constantly for ways to enhance that impression.

Reference

The origins of the 4Ps are unknown. There are many articles on the 4Ps on the internet.

Bilateral brain theory

The big picture

Understanding the functionality of the two hemispheres of the brain can help us to communicate more effectively with others. The right side of your brain controls the left side of your body and vice versa – for example, anyone unfortunate enough to suffer a stroke in the right side of the brain is likely to encounter paralysis in the left side of the face or body. The two halves (hemispheres) of the brain are connected by a bundle of neural fibres, the corpus callosum, which acts as a bridge between the two halves.

Each side of the brain appears to be responsible for separate functions and behaviours:

Left side

- Language
- Logic and rational thinking
- Mathematics
- Sequencing/Linear thinking
- Computation
- Facts

Right side

- Music
- Creativity
- Art

- Facial awareness

- Spatial ability

- Holistic thinking

Knowing the functionality of each side of the brain can help you to enhance your ability to communicate effectively with others.

When to use it

Use this knowledge whenever you need to be particularly persuasive.

How to use it

Try a little experiment. Stand up and face a wall. Imagine that on the other side of the wall someone is saying malicious things about you. Turn your head to listen to what they are saying. Now try turning the other way and it is likely that it will feel less comfortable, physically, than it did to turn the first way. Just as you have a dominant hand (the one you write with), a dominant foot (the one you kick with) and a dominant eye (the one to which you might hold a telescope), so you have a dominant ear. First time, quite instinctively, you will have turned your dominant ear to the wall. It was more comfortable to turn your head the first way than the second way because every time someone said something that was of interest to you, you would have inclined your head slightly so that your dominant ear was uppermost, so you will have developed a little more flexibility in the neck muscles on one side than the other.

If you turned your left ear to the wall, you prefer to use the right side of your brain to process auditory information. Turning your right ear to the wall shows a preference for using the left side to process auditory information. You can use this information not only to learn more effectively but to influence others. Let's look first at communication with other people and then at your own learning.

Influential communication

Look again at the different functions of the brain's hemispheres, which will give you clues about how to structure conversations differently for right- and left-ear-dominant people.

If you notice that each time you talk to a team member they incline their head slightly so that the right ear is uppermost, tailor your conversation to the functions of the left brain. Speak logically and analytically, ensuring that when you argue a case you structure your conversation so that each logical step leads inexorably to a conclusion. Expect to be quizzed on detail and have the facts to hand.

If you notice that each time you talk to a team member they incline their head slightly so that their left ear is uppermost, tailor your conversation to the functions of the right brain. Be creative in the use of language, talk in big-picture, conceptual terms, be prepared for tangential discussions and introduce emotional elements into the conversation.

Final analysis

The better we understand ourselves and others, the more effectively we can communicate. Combine this knowledge of brain theory with other communication skills such as embedded commands, positive language and VAK preferences to develop a powerful toolkit of influential techniques.

References

Joseph, R. (2001) *The Right Brain and the Unconscious: Discovering the stranger within.* New York: Basic Books.

Olson, J. (2015) *The Whole Brain Path to Peace: Exploring the role of brain hemispheres in a polarized world,* 2nd edition. San Rafael, CA: Origin Press.

58 Embedded commands

This language construct is a tremendously powerful technique of language and tonality, which influences others' behaviour at a subconscious level.

The big picture

Wouldn't it be nice if we could influence others to do what we would like them to do, so that they believed they were acting on their own impulses? There are many language constructs which can effectively bypass the critical faculty of the conscious mind and address the unconscious mind directly. Embedded commands are perhaps the most powerful of these constructs, allowing us to utter seemingly innocuous sentences which change the way others think and act.

When to use it

Use embedded commands in situations when direct suggestion has not worked well or (ethically) when you want to influence someone who may not be immediately amenable to your suggestions. Use them to influence other people's actions or behaviour for their benefit.

How to use it

Consider how you naturally utter a command. In spoken English, commands are issued with a downward inflection. The musical cadence of a command moves from its starting note to a lower note. Try saying 'Sit down!' in two ways – first with the word 'down' on a higher note than the word 'sit', and second with the word 'down' on a lower note. The latter sounds and feels right.

The unconscious mind registers this inflective pattern as a command and responds accordingly. Sometimes, the conscious mind also registers the command, sometimes not.

We're polite people and we often avoid directive speech. Instead of saying 'Sit down now', we say, for example, 'Would you mind sitting down now?' Say this out loud and listen to the musical cadence. Our desire to be polite and to avoid sounding commanding often results in a higher pitched voice and greater modulation than we would employ in our normal speech. Although we may downwardly inflect the words 'down now', there is no implicit command in the sentence. The result may be that we have to ask someone several times to sit down. The other's conscious mind has heard the request, but at the unconscious level, the sentence creates no particular image or feeling to which they naturally respond, so they do nothing. Notice how often people don't appear to have 'heard' what you ask them to do.

There are four simple stages in creating an embedded command:

1 Think about the command words you would use if you were being directive. For example, 'Sit down now'.

2 Add some 'fluff' words (some call them 'weasel words') – words that don't alter the meaning of the sentence you are about to utter but add a tenor of politeness. For example, 'Why don't you . . .?' 'Why don't you sit down now?' is perfectly innocuous.

3 Mark out the command words so that they stand out a little from the rest of the sentence. Say the words 'Sit down now' just a little louder than the other words. If the listener is also watching you, gesture towards their seat as you utter the words 'Sit down now'.

4 Downwardly inflect the last three words, so that you are using the normal commanding tonality. The effect of the downward inflection and tonal marking of the words is registered in the unconscious mind as a command, and most people will respond to it immediately. The physical gesture makes the command even more irresistible. The example is trivial. The effect is powerful.

So the formula for creating simple embedded commands is:

- Fluff words *plus* command *using* downward inflection and tonal/physical marking.

At first sight this may appear terribly contrived, but in fact you use these constructs all the time. The formula is the result of observation of how people communicate effectively, rather than a contrivance to change your ways of communicating. If you can model the effective formula purposely, then you can create powerful communications with observable results.

Here are some more, simple examples. In each case, downwardly inflect the italicised words, giving them a little more volume than the other words in the sentence:

- 'Why don't you *have a look* at this now?'

- 'Will you *have a go* at this?'

- 'Did you know you can *do this* too?'

Final analysis

You may, on reading this, question whether the practice is ethical or simply manipulative. It may be argued that all relationships are manipulative at some level. If you know the things that make your boss happy and you do or say those things quite deliberately, are you doing so because you want your boss to be happy, because your life is easier when your boss is happy, or a combination of both? In a sense, it doesn't matter, because you have chosen to take an action whose result (manifested in someone else) you can predict with some accuracy.

Use embedded commands with integrity. Those listening to a well-formed language construct may still reject it, consciously or unconsciously. We cannot elicit any response that stretches individuals beyond their moral boundaries; whether or not their conscious minds have immediately registered the commands we have uttered, the unconscious will prompt the conscious should we suggest anything that is offensive or morally unacceptable.

Reference

Waicukauski, R.J., Epps, J. and Sandler, P. (2010) *The 12 Secrets of Persuasive Argument.* Chicago, IL: American Bar Association.

Locus of control (Weiner's attribution theory)

59

The more we believe we can control events affecting us, the better we can make choices for the benefit of ourselves and others.

The big picture

Bernard Weiner of UCLA developed a model to explain how we perceive our successes and failures in terms of what we believe caused them. To what extent do you feel in control of your fate? For example, if you fail an exam, you might complain that you had too little sleep the night before, that the examiner set questions that were not in the syllabus you studied, that you were unlucky on the day in the choice of questions available, that you didn't know enough about the topic, that your family had done nothing to support you educationally.

We attribute causes to events and these attributions may be based on task difficulty, effort, ability and luck. These four attributions are based on three 'causal dimensions' (possible root causes):

- **Stability**: the extent to which the causes may change over time. *'I have been unwell this week and would probably do better in my exam tomorrow, when I am feeling better.'*

- **Locus of control**: this attribution relates to the sources of control, which may be *external* to you or *internal*. *'I was unlucky in the choice of questions to answer in the exam paper'* (external) or *'I am just not sufficiently competent to pass this exam'* (internal). Internal failures can damage your self-esteem and successes can make you feel proud of yourself.

- **Controllability**: to what extent do you have control over the situation? This will have an effect on how you feel about it. If you fail at something out of your control, you may start to blame others (or the world in general) for it. *'I failed the exam because the teaching in this university is so poor.'*

It is easy to think that when you do something well, it was due to your skill, and when a colleague you dislike succeeds in the same area, it was due to luck. It is also easy to slip into *false attribution error.* Imagine that you see someone trip over a loose paving stone. Your immediate thought is that they were clumsy. You trip over the same paving stone and blame the local council (or whoever manages the local pavements) for not ensuring that the paving stones are properly laid.

When to use it

Whenever you perceive that you or a team member has succeeded or failed at something, use this framework to consider the real root causes, so that you can avoid blame and aid your own or someone else's development.

How to use it

A team member is struggling to understand something technically which most of his peers seem to understand. He searches for a reason ('causality') and believes that, although he has worked as hard as his peer group to understand it, he is too stupid to do so. In terms of Weiner's model, this lack of ability is internal, unstable and controllable – and the cumulative effect of these factors is to damage his self-esteem and confidence. Because his esteem is low, it begins to affect his other work and he builds a self-image of someone incapable of working at the right level within the team.

Another team member has been struggling to understand the same technical issue. She has always been quick to grasp ideas and so believes that her current issue is due either to lack of time invested in learning the concept or a lack of effort on her part. Like the first team member, the attributions here are internal, unstable and controllable. Far from being demotivated, she determines that she will understand the concept and returns to it, discusses it with her peers, reads more about it and practises its application until she understands it fully. Her overriding emotion is one of motivation.

In managing others in situations where they feel some sense of failure, use the model to help them to analyse what is inside and outside their locus of control and what is controllable. Help them to see how they can start to take back control where they had either felt they did not have any, or had not exercised it. Help them reframe their feelings so that what may have seemed an insurmountable problem can be divided into manageable chunks so that it appears more readily achievable.

If time (stability in this model) is an issue, help them to manage their time better using some of the tools in this book, and relieve them of some of their less immediately critical duties so that they can focus on success in the area that is troubling them. Monitor them sufficiently closely to see that they are making progress, without micro-managing (which tends to stifle learning).

Final analysis

One of the most difficult tasks for a manager is to create and sustain a motivating environment. A perceived failure for one person becomes a motivator to do better; the same perceived failure in another damages their self-esteem and self-confidence. You need to monitor your team constantly to understand their individual responses to success and failure.

Encourage those who are successful to repeat their successes and ensure that they do not become boastful and damage the confidence of others. Encourage those who feel they have failed to understand that the situation is temporary and help them to see the areas in which they can either assume or take back control.

Reference

Weiner's book . . .

Weiner, B. (1974) *Achievement, Motivation and Attribution Theory.* Morristown, NJ: General Learning Press

. . . is out of print and copies are exchanged at large multiples of the original cover price. There are many articles on the internet about his model.

60 Positive language

The big picture

Negatives are a trick of language – if you suggest something using negatives, it implants in someone else's mind the very image of the thing you don't want them to do. Not only does positive language reinforce positive behaviours but it positively affects the well-being of the recipient, whereas the cumulative effect of negatives can create stress.

If you say to a small child 'Don't run in the road', it's quite likely that the child will do precisely that. The child cannot experience a negative, and the positive image you have placed in the child's mind is of running in the road. One of the reasons that diets are unsuccessful is because the dieter, with great intentions to be good, declares: 'Today I'm going to be really good. I'm not going to eat cake and I'm not going to have any chocolate.' The images in the dieter's mind are of eating cake and having chocolate. As we try to talk ourselves out of something, the negatives in our speech have exactly the opposite effect.

When to use it

Whenever you want to influence or persuade someone, use positive language.

How to use it

Imagine you have a report to write, containing important recommendations about policies and practices at work. In the recommendations section you state every-thing in the negative, telling staff what they must not do. The effect is to implant in their minds the very image of the thing you do not want them to do. The reticular activating system (see Chapter 53) obediently ensures that they get/do what they focus on and nothing changes. Form recommendations in positive language, stating exactly what you *do* want people to do, without reference to anything you don't want them to do.

Our language is peppered with negative words, such as 'no', 'not', 'never', 'nothing' and all the negated verbs like 'isn't', 'couldn't', 'shouldn't', 'don't', 'won't', 'mustn't' and 'haven't'. Each time you find yourself about to use these words, pause for a second and think how you could utter your statement using only positive language.

If you want to contradict someone, avoid the word 'but'. Effectively it erases everything that precedes it. 'I hear what you are saying, but . . . ' implies that you are not listening. 'That's all very well, but . . . ' implies that all is far from well. Substitute 'and' for 'but'. The mind becomes very open to what follows 'and' in a way that it does not with 'but'. You can contradict someone and as long as you preface the contradiction with an 'and' instead of a 'but' they will tend to accept what you say after the 'and' as an extension of the discussion, even if it directly contradicts them.

There is a large body of evidence to suggest that, when a child is constantly exposed to negative language from its parents, it is constantly unwell. In workplaces where bosses consistently use negative language, sickness levels rise to way above national averages. It appears that negatives act as minor stressors (causes of stress) at the subconscious level and the cumulative effect on the listener is the same as the cumulative effect of any stressor – it damages the immune system and causes illness. So, if you want a happy and healthy workforce, use positive language!

Final analysis

The best influencers naturally default to positive language, changing their *buts* to *ands* and eliminating negative words. They make people feel good about themselves and naturally attract others towards them. Management is not necessarily about being popular and yet those who are popular tend to have higher performing, motivated teams. Watch your language and notice the effects on your team.

Reference

Charvet, S.R. (1997) *Words That Change Minds: Mastering the language of influence,* 2nd edition. Dubuque, IA: Kendall-Hunt Publishing Co.

61

Spheres of influence

The big picture

Spheres of influence is a simple tool to help you frame difficult situations to determine what is within your sphere of control, what and whom you can influence and
which aspects are entirely out of your control and influence. Did you ever lie awake
at night worrying about something? Try as you might you couldn't see what to do
to resolve a difficult situation or solve a particular problem. It may have been that
in reality there was absolutely nothing you could do about it, but your mind worked
overtime trying to find a solution.

In any situation we have three levels of influence (see Figure 61.1):

1 **Control**: those situations in which we can either be in control or take control
   (partially or completely).

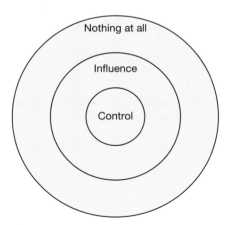

Figure 61.1 Spheres of influence

2 **Influence**: those situations in which we can influence someone so that we get closer to a resolution.

3 **Nothing at all**: those situations in which there is nothing we can do to control or influence an outcome.

When to use it

Use the model to help a team member who is struggling to resolve a problem or difficult situation.

How to use it

Help the team member to explain their situation or problem calmly and rationally in as much detail as possible. Ask about any personalities involved, helpers and constraints, the team member's current skills and knowledge, and the gaps in their skills and knowledge. Use 'dissociative' rather than 'associative' language – refer to *that problem* rather than *this problem*; discuss it in the past tense, as though it has already been resolved. Using dissociative language helps to distance the situation in the other person's mind so that they are able to discuss it more rationally than emotively.

Show them the model and work from the inside out, asking (now using associative language to make the solution seem closer and more real):

- What do you believe are the areas where you have some control here? (Be careful to distinguish between *controlling* and *being in control* – generally the latter is more useful.)

- Over whom do you/could you have some influence in this situation? (Help them to understand how they can exercise that influence.)

- Now, rationally, in which aspects of this situation is there nothing at all that you can do?

There is one area in which your team member can always exercise control – over their own behaviour. Show empathy and understanding of the team member's situation and acknowledge their feelings. Then coach them to understand the extent to which, while feeling as they do, they can still choose how they manifest that feeling on the outside to remain credible and professional.

Often, a story can help to illustrate to your team member the way the model might work in practice:

Imagine a driver, stuck in a major traffic jam. Cars are stopped as far as the eye can see. He learns from the local radio station that there has been an accident some way down the road and it may be an hour before the debris from the accident can be cleared away so that the traffic can move again. In a rage, he gets out of the car, climbs on a wheel arch and shouts at the traffic to get out of his way because he is in a hurry. Now what part of the traffic jam could he control?

[Nothing at all.] *What part of the situation could he influence?* [Nothing at all.] *What could he control?* [His behaviour, which served no purpose. Perhaps calling someone to say that he would be late.]

The aims here are to help the team member to:

- strip unhelpful emotion out of a situation and explore it rationally;

- become sufficiently resourceful in new situations to be able to deal with them calmly and rationally;

- understand the power of self-control and its effects on professional credibility;

- find the things that can be done so the team member feels they are exercising maximum control in a situation in which there appeared to be no solution.

Final analysis

Reinhold Niebuhr (1892–1971) captured the ideas here in his 'Serenity Prayer':

> *. . . grant me the serenity*
> *to accept the things I cannot change;*
> *courage to change the things I can;*
> *and wisdom to know the difference.*

Remember that you can apply most of the models and tools in this section to yourself as readily as to someone else. Use this tool to step back from something that concerns you and rationalise: are you investing too much energy in something you cannot influence or control? Is it worth the mental energy you are investing? Where could you channel that energy more positively to achieve a worthwhile result?

References

No references were found for this technique which, in various forms, has been a favourite among management trainers and coaches for many years.

[PART TWENTY]

Leadership

The age-old debate about the differences between leadership and management rages on. In essence, leaders have followers; good leaders have willing followers; great leaders have willing followers who follow them to do something good.

Whether or not you consider yourself a born leader, you can always improve your leadership skills. Here are some models to help.

Action-centred leadership

62

The big picture

John Adair developed the action-centred leadership model in the early 1970s while working at the Sandhurst Royal Military Academy and later at the Industrial Society in the UK. The model sets out the need to balance management of your team, the tasks they are undertaking and the individuals within the team, and demonstrates the interrelationships between them. It is often depicted as three overlapping circles (team, task, individual), a diagram which is trademarked to John Adair. Adair synthesised aspects of the motivational theories of Herzberg and Maslow in his work.

At any one time, you may need to shift from a focus on the team to a greater focus on the individual to a focus on the task to be accomplished.

Adair also identified six core principles of leadership, which are core to the action-centred leadership model: planning, initiating, controlling, supporting, informing, evaluating. He distinguished between leadership (giving direction) and management (managing the move towards that direction).

When to use it

Keep the action-centred leadership model in the back of your mind all the time when managing a team.

How to use it

As a manager you should be considering constantly where the primary focus of your attention needs to be. As you determine the area of focus, consider both your responsibilities in that area and the questions you need to ask yourself. Here are some indicative responsibilities and questions. The list is not exhaustive and will, to some extent, be context specific:

Area of focus	Responsibilities	Questions
Task	<ul><li>Set clear tasks.</li><li>Align tasks with group or organisational objectives.</li><li>Delegate.</li><li>Monitor progress against objectives.</li><li>Make resources (people, money, equipment, etc.) available.</li><li>Create a plan to help individuals and the team to achieve the task.</li></ul>	<ul><li>Does everyone understand what is expected of them?</li><li>Have I created a sufficiently good plan?</li><li>Is the working environment conducive to achievement of the task?</li><li>Does everyone understand their objectives in achieving this task?</li><li>Do we have the right resources?</li><li>Is the team the right size?</li><li>Does everyone understand their responsibilities and accountabilities?</li><li>Do we have sufficient time?</li><li>Who will cover in times of absence?</li><li>Am I the best role model I can be?</li></ul>
Team	<ul><li>Set and agree behavioural and performance standards.</li><li>Encourage team to achieve goals.</li><li>Ensure team is trained.</li><li>Manage conflict.</li><li>Build team morale.</li><li>Agree and develop roles within the team.</li></ul>	<ul><li>Does the team understand the standards that we will be working to?</li><li>Is this the best team composition?</li><li>Is the team the right size?</li><li>Does the team understand the code of behaviour expected?</li><li>Do the team members work cohesively as a team?</li><li>Does the team have a sense of its contribution to the broader organisation?</li></ul>
Individual	<ul><li>Understand individuals' motivations.</li><li>Recognise and praise effort.</li><li>Develop individuals.</li><li>Reward as appropriate.</li><li>Support and help individuals.</li></ul>	<ul><li>Is this the right person to do this job?</li><li>Does the team member know what is expected and have we agreed it?</li><li>Does the team member understand the organisation and the context for this work?</li><li>Does the team member understand their responsibilities?</li><li>Is the team member trained and ready for this work and will it help them to develop?</li></ul>

Adair's model may look obvious and perhaps superficial at first sight, but there is a great deal of depth here. Consider first of all the focus on task. If you understand the strategy of your organisation, then you can be relatively comfortable that each task your team performs has some strategic purpose. If you do not understand the strategy, you will create a silo in which your team may be very focused on task, but the tasks have little relevance to the organisation and team members will not understand the ripple effects of their actions on other areas of the organisation.

Now consider the focus on team. To what extent can you consider the team an amorphous mass, which will respond to the same direction? What are the things you can do with the team that do not require individual attention? What does the team en masse need from you? Is the team really a team or simply a group of people working in the same workspace? Teams have shared goals or targets. What binds your team together as a team?

Now focus on the individuals. How well do you know and understand them as individuals? What do they need individually in addition to (or instead of) what they need as part of a team? What motivates them as individuals?

How can you ensure that you strike the right balance between the three elements? And importantly, how can you be sufficiently flexible to adapt constantly so that you fulfil all three requirements?

Final analysis

The action-centred leadership model offers a comprehensive guide to what's needed at each stage in leading a team and has much to offer managers who also assume some level of leadership role. The key here is to achieve the best balance between the three areas – task, team and individual – rather than focusing on the one you find easiest to manage.

Reference

Adair, J. (1979) *Action-Centred Leadership.* Ashgate, UK: Gower Publishing.

63 Covert leadership

The big picture

In the sixth century BC, the Chinese philosophical tract, the *Tao Te Ching,* was published. Although it is attributed to a single author, Lao Tzu, the author's name translates as 'old man' or 'old master' and the likelihood is that it was the work of several people. Among its many themes are leadership and governance and its ancient principles can still be applied to modern-day leadership. Its 80 or so chapters are written in cryptic language and are still being interpreted.

Some of the passages are splendid introductions to covert leadership – the art of leading without appearing to lead:*

> *The wise person nourishes everything but does not claim it as his own,*
> *Works but doesn't take credit for it*
> *Leads but doesn't control:*
> *This is called profound virtue.*
> Chapter 10

> *When the leader has a light touch*
> *The people will be genuine and simple.*
> *When the leader has a heavy hand*
> *The people will be restless and needy.*
> Chapter 58

> *Ruling a state is like frying a small fish.*
> Chapter 60

> *And so the wise man leads his people without hindering them,*
> *He leads without obstruction,*

*All translations by the current author.

Therefore the world is happy to praise him
And never tires of him because he does not go against the flow
And no-one finds reason to contest him.
Chapter 66

The message running through all these verses is that the best leader is the one who prepares the ground and then stands back and allows his team to do the work. Micro-management is counter-productive.

Perhaps the most difficult passage to understand is from Chapter 60 – *Ruling a state is like frying a small fish.* The good chef cleans and seasons the fish, heats the oil to the right temperature, puts the fish in the oil and then *leaves it.* He monitors it by sight, sound and smell but does not touch it. When the fish is cooked on one side, he gently flips it over and again, leaves it. The result is a perfectly fried fish.

The bad chef does not clean the fish well, seasons it badly, does not heat the oil to the right temperature, then pokes and prods the fish as it is cooking. The result is a badly cooked fish, which falls apart.

Covert leadership is the art of knowing when to intervene and when to stand back, how to create the best working environment, in which people are both motivated to undertake a piece of work and sufficiently skilled to do it well.

An orchestral conductor is a prime exponent of covert leadership. The conductor prepares the orchestra through rehearsals to the point at which they understand precisely how she wants them to interpret the music. At the performance she ensures, with gestures alone, that the orchestra works to the plan and her minimal intervention at this stage produces beautiful music.

When to use it

Covert leadership is as much a philosophy of good management and leadership as a single tool. Apply it in all your thinking about how you manage and lead others.

How to use it

To practise covert leadership you must:

- ensure that staff are properly trained;
- establish clear (SMART) objectives and responsibilities;
- establish trust between you and the team and between team members;
- demonstrate that trust in your team;
- contextualise the work to be done in terms of organisational need;
- ensure understanding when you delegate work;

- know your team members' strengths and weaknesses;
- give encouragement and support;
- give recognition for a job well done.

In essence, you must do all the things that good managers are supposed to do, then step back and let the team take care of the work.

Consider the care that was taken to recruit your team. The likelihood is that you recruited your team members not only because they seemed a good fit for the vacant roles but because they were capable of thinking for themselves. Too often, when someone is recruited to a new organisation we deny them any initiative or freedom of thought. How do you imagine it feels to start a new job with real excitement and enthusiasm, only to have it crushed by micro-management which suggests that you cannot be trusted to do the job?

Covert leadership is about finding the appropriate balance between intervention and laissez-faire. How much help does the individual or team need? To what extent can you leave them to think and act for themselves? The covert leader should be confident in the team's ability, building their skills and leaving them to demonstrate them.

Final analysis

A word of caution: you may need to be careful when you practise covert leadership. In many organisations you will be judged as much by what you are seen to be doing as by the results your team achieves. Too much of what may appear a laissez-faire attitude may be ill judged by others around the organisation and even by members of your own team who don't understand your methods. To balance this, it is not helpful to talk too much about your philosophy – far better to demonstrate it. If you are encouraging, approachable and trusting, you can make it work. You may see the covert leader as a good waiter: always available when needed but never intrusive or overbearing. The waiter ensures that you enjoy the meal, but is not invited to the table to dine with you!

References

The following is just one of many translations of the *Tao Te Ching*:

Addiss, S. and Lombardo, S. (translators) (1993) *Tao Te Ching.* Indianapolis, IN: Hackett Publishing Co, Inc.

Mintzberg, H. (1998) 'Covert leadership: notes on managing professionals', *Harvard Business Review,* Nov–Dec, 76(6): 140–147.

Leadership styles

64

The big picture

Daniel Goleman, best known for his work on emotional intelligence (see Chapter 19), popularised the idea of six distinct leadership styles which cover the whole spectrum of leadership. Each of us uses the styles in different proportions and the more flexible we can be in applying the most appropriate combination of styles in each situation, the more effective our leadership will be.

When to use it

This broad-ranging tool will enable you to get the best out of yourself and others at work.

How to use it

The starting point is to understand your leadership preferences, the benefits of each and the potential downsides. Then consider, in any new situation, which mix of styles will give you the best result or richest solution.

Read each statement in the questionnaire and score it according to the guidelines below. Best results are achieved by scoring each statement quickly and intuitively, rather than pondering each one at length. Transfer the scores to the grid that follows the questionnaire, then read the descriptions of the styles that match your highest scores.

Scoring

Against each statement, allocate a number of points (note that there is no score of **4**):

This is always true of me	**5** points
This is often true of me	**3** points
This is true of me 50% of the time	**2** points
This is largely untrue of me	**1** point
This is totally untrue of me	**0** points

1	My team members trust me implicitly.	
2	I spend a lot of my time getting buy-in to ideas from my team.	
3	I expect my staff to do as they are told, without questioning my motives.	
4	I am more interested in setting long-term goals than in being involved in detailed day-to-day work.	
5	I delegate challenging assignments, even if they will not be accomplished quickly.	
6	I would prefer that team members be happy in their work than spend my time correcting each fault.	
7	I exemplify all the standards that I expect from my team.	
8	I believe in investing time in people.	
9	I translate the company's strategy into terms that the team can understand.	
10	Employees who do not do what their managers tell them deserve to be reprimanded immediately.	
11	I work hard to create a strong sense of belonging for all the team.	
12	I think that we can all get a good deal of insight into an issue if we discuss it as a team.	
13	Work should be very task-focused.	
14	I spend time helping staff to identify their strengths and areas for development.	
15	I believe that decision making in the organisation should be top down.	
16	I give my team the leeway to take calculated risks and be innovative, once I have set out the direction they should take.	
17	I try to set a vision and get staff to come along with me in creating that vision.	

18	I am not convinced that the team will work with initiative if I don't demonstrate what to do and how to do it.	
19	I work hard to establish strong emotional bonds between myself and my team.	
20	I give plentiful instruction and feedback.	
21	I hold a lot of meetings with my team to ensure that they are happy with the way the team is working.	
22	I know what is best for my team and expect them to do what I ask.	
23	Collective decision making is the most effective form of decision making.	
24	I identify poor performers and demand more from them.	
25	If staff do not perform well enough I believe they should be quickly replaced.	
26	If I believed that an existing system was restricting good work, I would have no hesitation in getting rid of it.	
27	In giving feedback, I look at the extent to which an individual's work has furthered the group vision.	
28	I encourage staff to create long-term development goals.	
29	I give my team members regular feedback on their performance.	
30	I set out where I want the team to get to, and expect them to use their initiative in getting there.	
31	I believe that we can always find ways to do things better and faster.	
32	I make agreements with my team members about their roles and responsibilities in enacting development plans.	
33	I give the team freedom to achieve our goals.	
34	I believe in letting the team have a say in the way that the team is managed.	
35	I have great self-control and expect to use my initiative alone in managing others.	
36	I think that team members should have a say in setting goals and objectives.	

Analysis

Transfer your scores from the statements above to the appropriate statement numbers in the grid below to determine your leadership style(s). For example, if you scored 5 for question 16, write 5 against question 16 in the second column below. Then add each column to get your scores.

Directive	Visionary	Affiliative	Participative	Pacesetting	Coaching
3	**4**	**1**	**2**	**7**	**5**
10	9	6	12	13	8
15	16	11	21	18	14
22	17	19	23	24	20
26	27	29	34	25	28
35	30	33	36	31	32
Totals					

Your primary score is the highest score from the columns above, and your secondary score is the next highest. These are your preferred, predominant management styles.

Understanding the styles

Directive ('Do as I tell you')

Directive leaders expect compliance from their team members. Whether or not they express their demands politely, they are clear in giving instructions and do not expect to be challenged. The style is most useful in times of crisis, when short deadlines are to be met and when action is needed immediately. It is, with pacesetting, the least popular of the leadership styles and often the lowest-scoring style in the assessment. Directive management has become unfashionable in many cultures. The people-focused styles (coaching, participative and affiliative) have grown in popularity.

- **Qualities of the directive leader**: articulate, self-confident, good judge of others' strengths and weaknesses, concise, direct.

- **Caution**: be careful not to over-use this style. It can seem cold and aggressive.

Visionary ('This is where we are, this is where we want to be – you're all adults, so now go and do it')

Visionary leaders are big picture, strategic thinkers. Charismatic and articulate, they are able to inspire others with their vision of how things might be. At the organisational level, the style is most useful when the organisation needs a morale boost.

- **Qualities of the visionary leader**: charismatic, articulate, confident, engaging, inspiring.

- **Caution**: if they misjudge a situation, visionary leaders may be perceived as self-publicists, out of touch with a team. There is a danger, too, that although they present an inspiring vision for the future, their teams do not have the wherewithal to put their vision into practice.

Affiliative ('You're all my friends, so let's help each other')

Affiliative leaders promote harmony within a team, always putting people first. They are highly approachable, have great empathy and are good relationship builders. The style is particularly useful in creating a good team spirit and bringing together people in conflict. Often the style is adopted by people who have been a team member and are then promoted to manage their peers. This can cause severe problems because the affiliative leader shies away from giving feedback that team members may find negative or hurtful because the leaders feel as though they are slapping old friends in the face.

- **Qualities of the affiliative leader**: approachable, empathetic, sincere, honest, fun, open.

- **Caution**: affiliative leaders can allow problems to escalate and poor performance to go unchecked because they do not want to hurt anyone's feelings. A team may feel that their leader gives too little direction, because the leader does not want to interfere with what the team members are doing. Affiliative leaders can be indiscreet, trusting that things they have said in confidence will remain confidential.

Participative ('Let's get everyone's buy-in before making a decision')

Participative leaders seek group consensus before implementing a solution. They can be strongly persuasive, influencing people behind the scenes so that, when the team meets, it quickly comes to an agreement. They are highly collaborative and good at getting buy-in from others. The style is most useful when a solution relies on mutual agreement.

- **Qualities of the participative leader**: persuasive, good meeting managers, collaborative, egalitarian.

- **Caution**: participative leaders often live in meetings, going from one to another and creating action points which they have no time to carry out. Rather than being decisive themselves, they may rely too much on others' opinions and so never reach a decision, which can be hugely frustrating for those working with them.

Pacesetting ('Follow me!')

Imagine that you are technically very strong in your own area. As a reward for technical excellence you are promoted to a managerial or supervisory position. A team member is struggling with something and your reaction is to go back to your first love – roll up your sleeves and demonstrate how to fix the problem. This is fine in that it shows the team member how it is done. However, it may do little to help the team member to work self-sufficiently by gaining personal experience of fixing the problem.

- **Qualities of the pacesetting leader**: dynamic, fearless, technically excellent.

- **Caution**: the pacesetter is quick to demonstrate how to solve a problem, but this may either send the message that team members are not to be trusted to work on their own initiative, or slow their progress in learning to do things for themselves. It is easy to say 'follow me – I'll show you how to do it – now you do it' and forget that the team member may not know how to do it. It is important to combine pacesetting with other styles, such as coaching, to help team members to think and act for themselves.

Coaching ('How would you do it?')

Coaches are concerned for the professional development of their staff and demonstrate great self-awareness, awareness of others and empathy. They listen well and ask good questions, helping their staff to find answers to their own problems and, ultimately, to work towards self-sufficiency.

- **Qualities of the coaching leader**: empathetic, egoless, good listener and open. Coaching leaders emphasise the professional growth of employees. They develop staff for the future. They demonstrate both empathy and self-awareness. This style is most useful in helping an employee to improve their performance or develop long-term strengths. It produces positive results where a team is keen to learn and develop.

- **Caution**: the coaching style is the rarest of all in modern business. Though much is said and written about coaching, it is not widely practised. While it does produce results, it does not make sense to staff members who have no desire to learn or change their practices. It also fails if the coaching manager lacks expertise.

Final analysis

The law of requisite variety in the field of cybernetics states: 'The larger the variety of actions available to a control system, the larger the variety of perturbations it is able to compensate.' Translate this into leadership terms and it reads: 'The wider the variety of styles the leader is able to demonstrate, the longer that leader will survive.'

The best leaders are flexible, able to adapt their style to the situation in hand and work through a variety of styles to achieve excellence. Once you know your preferred style, you can begin to practise others until they become part of your natural leadership vocabulary.

References

Goleman, D. (1996) *Emotional Intelligence: Why it can matter more than IQ.* London: Bloomsbury Publishing.

Goleman, D., Boyatzis, T. and McKee, A. (2002) *Primal Leadership: Learning to lead with emotional intelligence.* Boston, MA: Harvard Business School Press.

PART
[TWENTY-ONE]

Negotiation

We negotiate every day. Whether formally or informally, every time you and someone discuss something in order to reach mutual agreement, you are negotiating. Tradition has it that the aim of negotiation is to achieve a 'win-win', but this allows the possibility of someone losing. We win and lose games, battles and wars, but if we enter a negotiation in a spirit of 'winning' we may appear adversarial from the outset.

Modern thinking is that negotiation is *collaborative problem solving* or issue resolution, rather than confrontation. That said, at some stage in a negotiation, you may find yourself bargaining and, as you'll see, distributive bargaining, described below, is still known in many circles as the *adversarial* model of negotiation. This is counterbalanced by the two models that follow it – integrative bargaining and Harvard principled negotiation. Finally, we introduce RADPAC, which gives an overall framework for an effective negotiation.

Distributive bargaining (adversarial model)

65

The big picture

Distributive bargaining is a model of negotiation which involves bargaining over shares of a finite resource (money, land, etc.). Distributive bargaining, also described as 'win-lose' or 'zero-sum' negotiation, is a form of negotiation used to divide a finite asset into pieces to be distributed between the negotiating parties. In this form of negotiation one side's win is another side's loss.

Imagine a pie is to be divided between two parties, each determined to take the larger share (see Figure 65.1). At best they can take half each; at worst, one takes the whole pie. After bargaining, one takes a larger slice than the other. The owner of the bigger piece is happy. The owner of the smaller piece leaves feeling cheated.

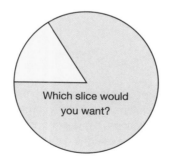

Figure 65.1 Distributive bargaining

When to use it

Distributive bargaining may be a part of an integrative negotiation at the point at which a finite resource must be divided, and should be managed with caution because of the danger of creating a win–lose and antagonising one of the other parties involved.

It tends to be used when the major parties in the negotiation do not understand the underlying issues. If you negotiate purely on 'position' ('I want X') rather than underlying need ('If I had X, I could . . .') then you are likely to find yourself involved in distributive bargaining.

How to use it

Imagine that a group of workers campaigns for a 5 per cent pay increase. The management holds out for 2 per cent. They bargain with each other and finally settle for something in the middle, say 3.5 per cent. Effectively the management team has given 1.5 per cent more than they wanted to offer and the workers have accepted 1.5 per cent less than they had hoped for. Neither is particularly satisfied with the result. The problem was in the starting point for the negotiation. Rather than discovering why the workers wanted/needed 5 per cent more, they simply haggled over a percentage pay increase. Had they dug deeper in their initial conversations, they might have been able to negotiate more creatively to meet the underlying need of the drivers, for example through the provision of benefits or better terms and conditions for the workers.

This may suggest that distributive bargaining is never a useful ploy. Realistically, there are times when you will have no choice but to bargain in this way. A standard tactic when distributive bargaining is unavoidable is to split the difference and then split the split in your favour. Let's see how this works in the context of simple market stall haggling:

At a market, you see a bag you like. The market trader tells you she wants 100 (of whatever currency you are negotiating in). You offer 50. The trader splits the difference and asks for 75. You split the split – approximately halfway between 50 and 75 – and offer 62. The bag is yours.

Final analysis

Treat distributive bargaining with considerable caution. If you find yourself drawn into it, consider taking time out to determine whether you truly understand the concerns of the other side. Ask more questions, dig deeper and try to discover what brought them to their current position by unearthing the underlying interests behind the negotiation so that you can move away from distributive bargaining to more collaborative integrative bargaining (see below).

Reference

Shell, G.R. (2006) *Bargaining for Advantage: Negotiation strategies for reasonable people,* 2nd edition. New York: Penguin.

Integrative bargaining

66

The big picture

Integrative bargaining, unlike distributive bargaining, does not aim to slice a finite 'pie' into pieces but to enlarge the pie or enable the negotiating parties to create joint value. There are four key principles in the process:

1 Identify the parties' shared interests.

2 See the negotiation as a business deal instead of a dispute.

3 Explore hidden attitudes.

4 Focus on the future.

When to use it

Use the principles of integrative bargaining in any negotiation in which distributive bargaining is not an absolute necessity. See also Harvard principled negotiation (Chapter 67), which extends this model.

How to use it

Each of the principles is designed to change your mindset as a negotiator so that you move away from the concept of dividing a finite resource between negotiating parties towards collaborative problem solving. Here is a particularly useful tool to make that shift.

You are about to negotiate with another party around an issue which, at first sight, appears to force you into distributive bargaining. Each party comes to the negotiation with a position: they know what they want in the ideal world and have some idea of what they can expect, realistically.

Negotiation around the ideal and the realistic is pure distributive bargaining and allows for no creativity in resolving the problem. If you are unable to agree on positions, effectively you have nowhere else to go in the discussions.

Imagine this: X wants a 5 per cent pay rise (ideal) and Y wants to give nothing (ideal). In reality, X expects a pay settlement between 0 per cent and 5 per cent at, say, 2.5 per cent (realistic), but Y stubbornly refuses to offer more than 1.5 per cent (realistic). The negotiations break down.

Each side needs to introduce a third element, the best alternative to negotiated agreement (BATNA). Traditionally, negotiators talked of an ideal, realistic and fallback, but the 'fallback' somehow suggested failure. The BATNA puts a more positive spin on the negotiations by offering space for creative solutions which take into account the shared interests of the two parties (principle 1 of integrative bargaining).

In preparing an integrative negotiation, sketch out the following:

	Your side	Their side
Ideal	The ideal solution for your side.	What you believe to be the ideal solution for their side.
Realistic	The realistic solution for your side.	What you believe to be the realistic solution for their side.
BATNA (best alternative to negotiated agreement)	An alternative solution, based on the shared interests of the two parties, which is measured either in a different 'currency' from the ideal and realistic or measured only partially in that 'currency', e.g. in a pay dispute, the positions are around percentage pay increases (the 'currency' is fixed monetary amounts or percentages) but a BATNA may be, for example, part money and part change in terms and conditions of service.	

Imagine that you are party Y in our pay dispute. You hold the purse strings and your workers are demanding a 5 per cent pay rise. You might sketch this:

	Your side	Their side
Ideal	0%	5%
Realistic	2%	2.5%
BATNA (best alternative to negotiated agreement)	1% this year An additional 1% next year Introduction of flexible working hours Job sharing for part-time workers	

The BATNA creatively explores the underlying interests that prompted the parties to come to the negotiating table. It allows discussion around the real issues, instead of the presenting issues. Think of a good negotiator like a doctor: a patient shows the doctor that he has a rash on his hand and the bad doctor prescribes an oint-ment that is for symptomatic relief; a good doctor examines the patient and treats the underlying causes of the rash. The good negotiator looks beyond the superficial presenting 'symptoms' ('I want a 5 per cent pay increase') and seeks to understand what brought the other patient to the negotiating table.

You will notice that in the examples given here, the BATNA cuts across both columns because it is a collaborative solution, which works equally for both sides and in so doing fulfils integrative bargaining principles 2 and 4 (See the negotiation as a business deal instead of a dispute and Focus on the future).

Principle 3 (Explore hidden attitudes) is the most difficult to manage during a negotiation. You cannot know exactly what the other side thinks of you, what preju-dices, whether realistic or ill-founded, they may hold, or what discussions they have had with each other prior to the negotiation. This means that, during the negotia-tion, you must listen intently, ask questions that get to the heart of the underlying interests without antagonising the other side, be open to reasoned arguments and flexible in creating solutions. The better you know the other side and their interests before the negotiation, the better you can start to draft a BATNA that truly works for both sides. This suggests that much of the best work should take place before you begin formal negotiations.

Final analysis

The examples here have been based around a pay dispute, because it provides a simple basis for discussion of the principles of integrative bargaining. As a manager, many of your negotiations will be less formal and often based around, for example, trying to increase the budget for your team, getting permission to recruit additional staff, buying new equipment or establishing service level agreements. The principles are the same: look beyond the obvious and understand the other side's underlying interests and then the creation of an ideal and realistic BATNA becomes far easier. Once you understand their interests, you enter into the negotiation with a collaborative mindset, because you have already begun to explore solutions that will appeal to both parties, without any spirit of competition and no need to achieve a 'win-win' because there was no fight in the first place.

Reference

Fisher, R. and Ury, W. (2012) Getting to Yes: Negotiating an agreement without giving in. London: Random House Business.

67

Harvard principled negotiation

The big picture

Harvard principled negotiation provides a framework for integrative bargaining. It was designed by Harvard Professor Roger Fisher and William Ury, Distinguished Harvard Fellow, as a method of negotiation which would preserve excellent business relationships through 'wise agreement'.

It is based on four simple principles:

1 Separate the people from the problem.

2 Focus on interests, not positions.

3 Invent options for mutual gain.

4 Insist on objective criteria.

It moves away from negotiation as confrontation towards negotiation as collaboration.

When to use it

Use these principles in any negotiation in which distributive bargaining is not absolutely necessary.

How to use it

1 Separate the people from the problem

It is all too easy to allow mutual distrust or dislike of the other party to cloud our judgement in negotiation. It is important to separate the issue being negotiated from the people around the negotiation table. If you do not like the other party, then acknowledge this to yourself, set that thought to one side and focus on the issue to be resolved. If you allow your feelings about the other party to become important, you will not be able to negotiate rationally and objectively. Work hard to develop rapport with the other party; reframe your feelings about them, perhaps asking what you could learn from them; focus your planning efforts on the central issues, not the people.

Put yourself in the other party's shoes and see the negotiation from their perspective. As you do so, you should find that it dilutes any hostility you may feel towards them. Listen intently to what they are saying and summarise your understanding before responding. Listen with attention and speak with intention.

2 Focus on interests, not positions

In negotiation we talk about what someone asks for at the outset as their 'position'. Your team member asks for a 10 per cent pay increase: this is a position, the thing they have decided upon before the negotiation takes place. Any negotiation based around the pay increase will be haggling over percentages – distributive bargaining. Try to discover why the team member asked for this specific amount, why she needs this particular amount, what brought her to the point at which she felt she needed to ask for it. This is their 'interest', which caused them to decide upon their position. Rather than insisting on an absolute bottom line in your negotiations, explore the other person's interests and you will find you can create a wider range of mutually agreeable options.

3 Invent options for mutual gain

Rather than suggesting and doggedly sticking to a single option, create a wide range of options before you and the other party begin to select the ones that are mutually agreeable. Never reject an idea out of hand, but explore it to see whether buried within it is the germ of a positive solution.

Avoid fixing on a single solution, offering a solution too early without fully understanding the situation, believing that there is a finite 'pie' to be divided, failing to consider alternatives, pre-determining a solution and then steering the whole discussion towards it.

4 Insist on objective criteria

If you are able to put aside any personal animosity towards the other party and focus on the core of the negotiation, then you can approach the discussions more rationally and objectively. Work towards results that are based on entirely objective criteria, rather than being drawn into battles of will. If you need to concede something, do it based on pure principles rather than emotional pressure exerted by the other party and, through the negotiations, ensure that you are open to reason from the other party just as you reason objectively with them.

Final analysis

Critics of principled negotiation suggest that:

1 While one intention is to maintain long-term relationships, short-term considerations may sometimes overrule longer-term issues.

2 It can be difficult to get out of an impasse situation without short-term fixes.

3 Negotiators who set aside their feelings about the other party may never truly develop trust in each other, and the true basis for long-term relationships is trust.

4 The model does not take into account the possible levels of power, differing ideologies or political leanings of each party which may shift the balance in the negotiations.

While there is certainly validity in these criticisms, perhaps the critics overlook the important word in the title, 'principled'. The Fisher and Ury framework is not a prescriptive set of rules for negotiation but a high-level set of principles which attempts to guide the negotiator towards a rational and ethical stance. Adapt the framework to your circumstances.

Reference

Fisher, R. and Ury, W. (2012) *Getting to Yes: Negotiating an agreement without giving in.* London: Random House Business.

RADPAC

68

The big picture

An ill-prepared negotiation can be disastrous. At best it becomes a loose, unfocused conversation and at worst, an unpleasant confrontation. RADPAC provides a simple framework for negotiating:

- **R**apport/relationship building
- **A**nalysis
- **D**ebate
- **P**roposal
- **A**greement
- **C**lose

When to use it

Use RADPAC to frame any relatively formal negotiation.

How to use it

Let's look at each element in turn.

Rapport/relationship building

The extent to which you expect to talk socially before a more formal negotiation varies between cultures. It is a useful stage in the process, giving time for you to assess the other parties involved and create a positive impression. If you can set a good tone at this stage, you may expect a more collaborative approach during the negotiation.

Analysis

Now that you have begun the more formal negotiation, use this stage to test your understanding of the other side, establish some facts, understand the other side's feelings and express your own. If you could simply agree on something, you would not need to negotiate. Through this analysis, you can understand better the reasons for the negotiation and the basis on which you can work towards agreement.

Debate

The word 'debate' suggests two forces in opposition, trying to convince each other of the rightness of their approach. In good negotiation, the debate stage is about searching for *mutually agreeable solutions*, with constant summarising and checking understanding so that the sides move together to create a collaborative solution. Well handled, it can be a very positive stage.

Proposal

At this stage, one or more parties should be suggesting viable, mutually agreeable options as either a complete or a partial solution to the area of negotiation. It is important to listen well to the other side's proposals: even if they do not exactly match your initial thinking, there may be the seed of a solution there which you can help to develop.

Agreement

The agreement stage starts with a restatement of what you have agreed during the proposal stage, and allocation of people and time limits to the achievement of the solution. Record the agreement, read it back to everyone and confirm that it is correct.

Close

The close stage should be a very positive stage, which leaves the door open for future negotiation through confirmation of agreement and discussion of what you have mutually achieved through the negotiation. Thank the other side for giving their time to the negotiation and agree any follow-up steps.

Final analysis

RADPAC succeeds through simplicity. Be careful not to move through the stages too quickly. If it is useful to spend more time on social talk before analysis or to do more analysis before making concrete proposals, then this is time well spent. It is far better to keep moving forward in a negotiation than to have to backtrack because something vital was missed at an earlier stage.

Reference

The origin of RADPAC is unknown and there appear to be no books specifically devoted to it. The internet sites which describe it are often almost word-for-word copies of each other. This chapter is probably as comprehensive as any other guide to the process.

PART
[TWENTY-TWO]

Presentation

Every time you speak and mention your organisation's name in the same breath, you are presenting and your credibility may rise or fall according to your ability to present well. There is no escaping presentation and with increased seniority the pressure grows to speak and present well publicly, talk articulately at meetings and represent your organisation professionally.

69

INTRO

The big picture

Audiences don't care about speakers. While you may be nervous about presenting, typically the audience has not given a second thought to you until you stand up to present. Even then, you have to exaggerate your nerves before the audience really starts to take notice of them. So, while the audience may not be on your side when you present, its members are generally neutral towards you.

People remember the first and last things you say ('the law of primacy and recency') and if you can get the introduction to your presentation right, the audience will be much more forgiving if the main body of the presentation is a little dull!

The INTRO mnemonic is a wonderful model for constructing the opening of a presentation. INTRO stands for:

- **I**nterest/**I**mpact
- **N**eeds
- **T**iming
- **R**ange
- **O**bjectives

When to use it

If you write out no other part of your presentation verbatim, do write the introduction, using the INTRO mnemonic. It will act as a comfort blanket, giving you great confidence that you have a strong start to your presentation. Learn it by heart and whether or not you use notes as a further comfort, you'll find that it boosts your confidence from the outset.

How to use it

Many presenters begin by giving their name and the topic they are about to present. This is dull and bores audiences. The likelihood is that they know who you are and what you are planning to talk about, and if this is your first statement to them, you may lose them at the outset.

In planning the Interest or Impact stage, think of something that will grab their attention and make them sit up and think or examine their own experience. You might ask a question, make a challenging or provocative statement, or draw attention to something topical which you can weave back into the presentation later. If you can find a good question which forces the audience members to reflect on their history or experience, it deflects attention from you, and if you are a nervous presenter, this can help enormously because you are not the centre of attention in those opening moments. As audiences reflect on a question that taps into their personal experience, so they engage better with the subject and see its relevance to them from the start.

The Needs stage is designed to show the audience why it should be important for them to listen to you. Don't tell them explicitly that they need to listen, but make it clear to them through what you say and how you deliver it that they can benefit from listening.

At the Timing stage, tell them how long the presentation will be.

Range tells them the scope of the presentation – the main themes that you intend to address.

Finally, Objectives tells them what they will take away with them that they did not have at the outset.

Make sure you follow the sequence of INTRO. If you start by telling your audience that you are going to be talking for an hour you may turn some of them off before they understand what you are going to say. If you engage them at the Interest and Impact stage, they will be happier to hear that it will take an hour to present your topic. If the Interest/Impact and Need stages are well presented they may even be disappointed that you have only an hour with them. It is always better that an audience feels that your presentation was too short rather than too long.

Here are a couple of examples. In the first, imagine that the presenter is making a presentation about presenting.

Interest/Impact: *'There is no escape! Every time you open your mouth to speak and utter this company's name in the same breath, you are presenting and, in that moment, you **are** the company. If those listening to you have never met anyone from this company before, they will judge the company based on your credibility and professionalism in presenting . . . '*

Needs: *' . . . and so, if you are going to present, it's imperative that you do it well.'*

Timing: *'Over the next 40 minutes . . . '*

Range: ' . . . I'm going to introduce you to tools and techniques to spice up the introduction to your presentations, make the middle memorable, and conclude with real impact . . . '

Objectives: ' . . . so that, when you leave here you will be vastly more confident in your ability to present credibly and professionally to others.'

You'll notice that the style is relatively conversational. Rather than stop and start at each stage of the INTRO, it flows seamlessly between them. This is important again in engaging the audience because it could easily appear mechanistic: 'I have five points to make in my introduction and here they are!'

Here's another, slightly sinister example. See if you can pick out each of the five elements of INTRO in this introduction. It's Monday morning and the Sales Director of the Widget Division in a factory that manufactures both widgets and wodgets is addressing her sales team:

Good morning, ladies and gentlemen. Our colleague, George Smith, alas no longer with us as of last Friday, went on Wednesday to sign up ABC Corporation to a shipment, he believed, of $100,000 of widgets. George had been with us a long time and had detailed knowledge of the world of widgets. When he arrived, he discovered that ABC was looking for a part shipment of widgets and a part shipment of wodgets. George, knowing nothing of our wodget capabilities, failed to close the deal and, as you have heard, is no longer with us. So, over the next 30 minutes or so, I am going to introduce you to the wonderful world of wodgets – our product range, pricing policy, lead time on delivery and discount possibilities – so that you will leave here confident in your ability to cross-sell, should you ever find yourself in the same situation as poor George.

Notice that the need here is implicit rather than explicitly stated.

Final analysis

INTRO is probably the most effective structure for introducing a presentation. Even when you are asked to give an impromptu presentation, keep the mnemonic in mind and create it as you speak.

Reference

There are no known published references for this model.

PART
[TWENTY-THREE]

Relationships

Your ability to build and maintain relationships is a crucial element of your management practice. There is a great deal of evidence to support the idea that the people with the best networks are the most productive people, because they always know who to ask when they need something and their networks will support them in fulfilling their needs.

Management is not simply top-down – you need to develop and manage peer relationships and also manage upwards, anticipating your boss's needs and being ready to deliver when asked. In this part you'll find some models that will help you to think about your current working relationships and ways of enhancing them.

The four agreements (Ruiz)

70

The big picture

The Toltecs of Southern Mexico were the cultural and intellectual predecessors of the Aztecs. The Toltec masters, known as *naguals,* were scientists and artists who wanted to conserve ancient wisdom. *Naguals* followed shamanistic practices of attaining altered states to communicate with a spirit world. Don Miguel Ruiz was a Mexican surgeon who, following a near-fatal car accident, trained as a *nagual.* According to Ruiz, we learn through a process of reward and punishment and, in time, begin to fear the punishment and fear the lack of reward. We become a copy of the beliefs of our parents, society and perhaps our religion. Ruiz calls this process *domestication.* We develop an inner Judge, which tells us that we have broken the rules of domestication, and an inner Victim, which carries guilt and shame. We can convince ourselves that we are not good enough, and the Judge and Victim concur.

We have agreed to the codes set for us by our parents and society – we live by these *agreements.* When we remember our past transgressions, we feel guilty and so continue to punish ourselves for mistakes. Ruiz claims that the *agreements* to which we have subscribed are fundamentally wrong. We have based much of our belief on fear and created our own hell. We live in a perpetual dream, called *mitote* by the Toltecs, and the *mitote* prevents us from seeing who we truly are. We create an image of perfection and then cannot live up to it, because the image is not real, but we wear social masks to hide the real us. We only walk away from people who abuse us more than we abuse ourselves.

Our agreements with ourselves tells us what we are, what we believe, what we can and cannot do, what is reality, fantasy, possible and impossible.

The four agreements are powerful agreements, which are designed to replace the faulty ones to which we already subscribe and create a new code for living that will enhance our personal relationships, our personal development and the effectiveness of our communication with others. The four agreements are:

1 Be impeccable with your word.

2 Don't take anything personally.

3 Don't make assumptions.

4 Always do your best.

When to use it

Ruiz presents neither a quick fix nor a magical solution to relationship issues, but a philosophy which, though easy to understand in principle, will take considerable time to absorb and practise. If you find it appealing, practise each element in turn until it becomes a natural part of your behaviour.

How to use it

Agreement 1: Be impeccable with your word

Ruiz says that the first agreement is the most important. The 'word' refers not simply to sounds or written symbols but to your power to express yourself, to communicate with others, to think and so have control over the events you create in your life. When we tell someone what we think of them, we can walk away, but they may continue to dwell on what we say and it can have long-lasting harmful effects on them. A child branded stupid at school finds ample evidence to support the idea and grow up feeling stupid – the words become a self-fulfilling prophecy. Finding someone who is prepared to tell the child (or later, the adult) that they are not stupid may later break the spell.

What we tell ourselves can have equally powerful effects on our well-being and state of mind. We have the ability to choose what we say and do and we should use it wisely.

Being impeccable with your word means 'doing so without sin' – in practical terms, taking responsibility for yourself and your actions, without judging or blaming yourself. Whatever we do creates reactions in others. If you are nice to someone, they are likely to reciprocate. If you are unkind, they may be unkind to you.

Think of the way you talk to your team members at work. How often have you allowed yourself to show anger or displeasure instead of remaining calm and rational? How often have you felt that someone was stupid and allowed that feeling to leak out in what you say and do not say? Acting impeccably, using your energy to bring about peaceful solutions brings instant and long-lasting rewards.

Agreement 2: Don't take anything personally

When someone says something unpleasant about us, our immediate reaction is to feel wounded or angry. The second agreement says that when you say something unpleasant about someone else, this is really about you, rather than them. Other people do not do things because of you – you are not the centre of their personal universe. They do what they do and say what they say for their own reasons.

If you label someone stupid, this is a reflection of your own beliefs, opinions and feelings. If someone is unpleasant to you, it is about their beliefs, opinions and feelings, and taking it personally creates a negative feeling in you, leading to a breach of the first agreement. Whatever someone else thinks is their problem, not yours. They see the world through a different lens – they live in their own dream, just as you live in yours. We cannot see the world entirely through someone else's eyes and so do not truly know what brought them to a point in their life where they felt justified in criticising you. Just as we lie to ourselves, others lie to themselves.

Ruiz says that even your own opinions about yourself are not necessarily true and so you don't need to take negative self-talk personally. You have a choice to believe or disbelieve your self-talk, but it is a mistake to assume automatically that it is true.

In taking things personally, you allow yourself to suffer for no good reason. Ultimately, not taking things personally can give you a great deal of personal freedom. You are not responsible for others, only for yourself.

If you are resolving conflict between two team members, try to get them to dissociate themselves from the emotion of the situation. Get them to focus on what each of them can do differently, rather than on how they can change the way they feel. If their argument revolves around how each makes the other feel, there is no solution because they will continue to feel the way they do, taking each other's words and actions personally and being aggrieved at them. Take a calm, rational approach, which divorces the conversation from personal animosity and steers them towards objective solutions based on actions.

Agreement 3: Don't make assumptions

Once we make an assumption, we can find all the evidence in the world to support it and the assumption becomes a belief, a part of the *mitote*. If we make assumptions and take things personally, our thinking becomes chaotic. We cannot assume that we know how others think; we cannot assume that others see life the same way as we do; we cannot assume that we can change other people, because we do not have responsibility for others, only ourselves.

Relationships are damaged by mistaken assumptions. Consider a time when there was conflict either between two team members or between you and a team member. Is it possible that those involved have assumed things to be true? If so, they will subconsciously have filtered in any data that supports the assumption and filtered out anything that counters it.

Assumptions are made to fit our entrenched beliefs. Rather than ask questions and draw a complete picture of a situation, we readily jump to conclusions based on scant evidence. We learned very early in our school careers not to ask questions for fear of being made to feel stupid and so we flesh out the bare bones of a story so that it fits with our world view.

Ask questions when you do not know something. Ensure that you have the most complete picture before taking action. Imagine that you have decided that one of your team members is exceptionally clever and another is particularly stupid. You will, whether consciously or not, treat each of them as though your assumptions are true, giving praise to the clever one and berating the stupid one. Meanwhile, you readily forgive the clever one when she makes a mistake and you fail to notice when the stupid one does something of merit. It does not take long before you are accused, with some justification, of favouritism. We are human and will inevitably have favourites among our team members. As a professional manager, you cannot afford to show that favouritism. Stepping right back to the origins of the favouritism, it may be based on assumptions created with little evidence.

Agreement 4: Always do your best

The fourth agreement reinforces the other three, and even standing alone might be a good mantra for a serious professional – always do your best. Your best will vary in quality according to circumstances, your mood, the complexity of the work and many other variables. Don't strive to do better than you can, but realise where your best performance lies and channel your energy into giving your best.

Doing your best means being productive, being good to other people, and implies action rather than passivity. When you do your best, you enjoy even the things you had not particularly wanted to do and so get lots of little rewards throughout the day. If you know you have done your best, you have no reason to judge yourself and the Judge and inner Victim remain quiet. Don't take action because you have to, but take action in order to do the best you can. Ruiz describes action as 'living fully'.

Final analysis

What may at first sight appear to be a rather New Age theory actually provides some solid guiding principles and is no more esoteric than Covey's immensely popular 7 habits (see Chapter 10). Like anything new, it takes considerable practice until it becomes second nature. Not taking things personally and not making assumptions are extraordinarily difficult skills to master, but constantly reminding yourself to step back from situations and reframe them rationally and unemotively is a powerful step in developing your professional credibility.

Reference

Ruiz, D.M. (author) and Mills, J. (ed.) (1997) *The Four Agreements: Practical guide to personal freedom.* San Rafael, CA: Amber-Allen Publishing.

Rapport building

The big picture

While the old adage that opposites attract may be true, long-term relationships tend to be established around common ground – shared interests, values and ways of thinking and behaving. When we meet someone else we send out subtle signals, picked up unconsciously by the other person, which suggest the extent to which we are similar to them. These may be conveyed through body language, voice tone or eye contact. Two people 'in rapport' may appear to mirror aspects of each other's body language or speech.

You can tell something about the relationship between two people as you observe them in conversation. Where one always leads in terms of new posture, gestures, etc. and the other follows, this suggests that each sees the first as the more dominant one in the relationship. If the first leads and the second follows, then the second leads and the first follows, this suggests that they see each other as equals in the relationship.

When to use it

Rapport building is an essential part of building good relationships.

How to use it

There are many ways to build rapport with someone:

1   **'Mirror' body language**: two people in rapport tend to reflect each other's gestures and posture. Each may sit with arms folded and legs crossed, for example, or use expansive arm gestures as they talk to each other. If you are naturally comfortable with another person, you will automatically match aspects of their body language; if you are not, you may find yourself mismatching it. Try mimicking some of the other person's gestures. Be careful here: if you copy someone else's gestures and they are not consciously aware that you are doing so, it can help to create rapport;

if they become consciously aware that you are copying them, it will break rapport. The trick is to copy their gestures on a smaller or bigger scale. For example, if they fold their arms, cross your wrists; if they cross their legs, cross your ankles. At the subconscious level, these will be interpreted as the same gesture, or sufficiently similar to create a sense of rapport – a feeling of 'you are like me and I am like you' – but they are sufficiently different that the other person will not be consciously aware that you are copying them.

2 **Mirror voice tone and tempo**: if the other person speaks quickly, match their speed; if they speak slowly, slow down. Don't imitate accent or dialect if yours and theirs do not naturally match. The FBI claims that this is the most effective rapport builder.

3 **Breathe in time with the other person**: when we are intimate with people we often breathe in time with them and to create some sense of intimacy we can synchronise our breathing with theirs. As the other person is speaking, they are breathing out. Their shoulders rise when they inhale and fall when they exhale. Synchronising breathing can work very quickly to create a deep sense of rapport.

4 **Show understanding**: by nodding, smiling and using verbal assent ('uh huh', 'oh?', etc.).

5 **Mirror the other person's language**: listen to what they say and use some of their phrases as you respond.

6 **Find common ground**: discover shared interests and passions.

7 If you mirror someone for a few minutes, then change something about your posture, gestures, voice tone, etc. and the other person follows you, at that point trust is established. Look out for this moment in negotiations or when you want to argue a particular point with someone. They will tend to be more receptive at the point at which they subconsciously start to mirror you.

Final analysis

The concept of rapport building is simple enough – if I think that you are like me, I will probably feel more comfortable with you than if you appear very different. Be careful not to see rapport building as an end in itself but as a useful starting point in building fruitful working relationships. As you practise rapport building, so you will have to focus intently on the other person. This increased attention will make the other person sense that you are really interested in them and this in itself will have the effect of building rapport and strengthening the relationship.

Reference

Dreeke, R. (2011) *It's Not All About Me: The top ten techniques for building quick rapport with anyone.* Robin K. Dreeke.

Transactional analysis

The big picture

Transactional analysis (TA) is a branch of popular psychology developed in the 1950s by Canadian psychoanalyst Eric Berne (1910–1970), which contends that in our relationships we approach each other from a variety of 'ego states', described as Parent, Adult and Child. Through an understanding of our own and other people's ego states we can communicate better and develop more effective relationships with others.

When two people meet, one will start to talk. What that person says is called the *transaction stimulus.* The other will respond with the *transaction response.* Each stimulus and response is said to come from one of the three ego states: parent, adult or child. It is important to note that the terms *parent, adult* and *child* as used in TA do not tally exactly with their definitions in common parlance.

Parent state

As a child, much of your direction came from grown-up people – parents, grand-parents, teachers and others who directed you with imperatives and strong suggestions, such as 'You can't . . .', 'Don't . . .', 'You mustn't . . .' or 'Stop that!' We learn 'never' and 'always' from these figures of authority. As we grow up, we mentally 'record' these statements and our *parent* state reflects these external influences on our upbringing. The parent in TA can be described as *nurturing* or *controlling.*

Child state

If the *parent* state is based on external influences as we grow up, so the *child* state is based on internal emotions and feelings. How did you feel when someone told you off, smiled at you, bullied you, disapproved or approved of you? We mentally record all these feelings and they shape our *child* state. The child in TA can be described as *natural* (little self-awareness, child-like noises, playful); *little professor* (curious and experimental); and *adaptive* (either adapting to their circumstances or rebelling against them). A combination of the *natural* and *little professor* gives us the *free child.*

Adult state

The *adult* state sits between the other two states and is created as we observe the differences between what we observed (*parent* state) or felt (*child* state). The *adult* draws conclusions independently, is rational, assertive and comfortable in their own skin, basing discussions around facts and data.

A stimulus from any one ego state may receive a response from the same or another (see Figure 72.1).

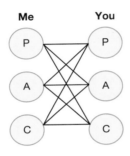

Figure 72.1 Transactional analysis

Source: After Berne, E. (1958) 'Transactional analysis: A new and effective method of group therapy', *American Journal of Psychotherapy*, 12(4): 735–43.

Three types of transaction are possible:

Complementary

Each addresses the other based on the state the other is in, e.g. adult to adult or child to child, parent to child.

- 'Have you had a chance to read the Board report?' (adult–adult)
- 'Yes, I am just looking at it now' (adult–adult)
- 'Do you think the boss will notice if we leave now and go for a drink?' (child–child)
- 'Brilliant idea! If we go out of the office the back way, we might get away with it' (child–child)
- 'I expect that report to be on my desk by 5pm' (parent–child)
- 'I'll finish it a lot quicker if you don't stand over me while I'm writing it!' (child–parent)

Crossed

Partners address each other in a different state from the one their partner is actually in. Conflict may ensue.

- 'Have you had a chance to read the Board report?' (adult–adult)

- 'I'll read it a great deal quicker if you stop phoning every five minutes!' (child–parent)

Ulterior

The surface-level conversation sounds reasonable, but there is a hidden ulterior motive. Berne describes these as the social message (what we said) and the psychological message (what we actually meant). When we are sarcastic, for example, the words are misaligned with the tonality and body language:

- 'I am sure that if we give you enough time you may prove competent' (adult–child) (Spoken with a smile, a sigh, arched eyebrows and head tilted down)

When to use it

Any time you are about to praise a team member, reprimand them, give them a difficult message, allocate work to them, appraise them – in any significant 'transaction' between you and a team member – use TA to frame your approach and responses.

How to use it

TA provides a wonderful insight into how we communicate and knowledge of it will help you to frame your own communication in any interaction with others. It will help you, too, in interpreting others' messages and responses to you.

Start by observing other people's conversations. Notice when they are easy and relaxed and when there is tension. Reflect on what happened. Which states were people working from? Were they complementary, crossed or ulterior? What could either of the participants in a crossed transaction have done differently?

Now think back to a recent, uncomfortable conversation at work. Did you open the conversation (transaction stimulus) or respond to someone else (transaction response)? From which ego states did each of you operate at the outset? Did you maintain those states throughout the conversation or did they change? If you could rewind and replay the conversation, what would you do differently? How could you apply knowledge of TA to reach a better or more comfortable outcome?

In dealing with conflict between team members, from which states are they operating? Can you, operating from the *adult* state, arbitrate in such a way that you demonstrate that your *adult* state moves them quickly to a solution?

When faced with someone speaking as a child, frame a response as an adult. Although this is a crossed transaction, it strips the emotion out of the conversation and sends a message that you will not enter into a child–child interaction. In removing the emotion, you will sound like the more mature person, rational and in control.

● Team member (petulantly): 'It's just not fair. You never give me any good projects.' (child)

● You (calmly): 'Let's talk about the work that's available at the moment and see which project you would like to undertake. We'll look at your current and projected workload and assess the time commitment you would need.' (adult)

● You (calmly): 'I notice that you have been using the internet a great deal for personal use during working time this week.' (adult)

● Team member (angrily): 'You can't prove that – it's just your word against mine.' (child)

● You (calmly): 'It's important that you focus on your core projects during the working day. I will ask the IT department to send me a log of your computer usage this week. Let's meet tomorrow at the same time and we can talk again then.' (adult)

Final analysis

Knowledge and practice of transactional analysis can boost your self-awareness as you learn how to frame conversations that work. It can also increase your awareness of others as you see how changing your own state affects them and as you observe what works and does not work in their relationships with each other, as viewed through a TA lens.

Reference

Berne, E. (2010) *Games People Play: The psychology of human relationships.* London: Penguin.

PART
[TWENTY-FOUR]

Teamwork

One of the core competencies in many organisations is teamwork. You will be judged on your ability to create a sense of bonding across your team and to work with others at all levels of the organisation. An understanding of team evolution and team dynamics can be helpful in assessing and developing your team skills.

Sigmoid curve

73

The big picture

The sigmoid curve (see Figure 73.1) graphically describes life cycles of almost anything and can be applied very simply to thinking about how to keep a team at its highest performance levels or scaled up to look at the overall organisation.

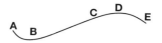

Figure 73.1 Sigmoid curve 1

Imagine Figure 73.1 as a chart for a commercial business and follow it from left to right. As the organisation is first established [A], little is happening, then products are developed, controls are put in place, marketing is developed, money and energy are expended and nothing has yet been produced [B]. The marketing is starting to work, the products are selling and the business performance picks up a momentum of its own [C]. In time, the product sales begin to decline, systems and processes may become outdated and performance levels off [D] and starts to decline [E]. (Look at Chapter 75 on the extended Tuckman teamwork theory and you'll see that it follows exactly the same curve.)

Let's look in more detail at points C and E – see Figure 73.2.

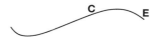

Figure 73.2 Sigmoid curve 2

While it is counterintuitive to fix something that is not broken, if we make no changes to the business until we reach point E, energy levels are low, morale may be in decline and cash flow may be a problem. So the best time to make a change is at point C. The effect is to create a second curve – see Figure 73.3.

Figure 73.3 Sigmoid curve 3

Inevitably, there will be disruption at point C and it may be a short time before things start to improve. Had we left the change to point E, it is conceivable that the line would have dropped considerably further before its upturn, and it would be much more difficult to bring the business back to high performance.

The sigmoid curve is especially useful in team management.

When to use it

Use the sigmoid curve to gauge when to make changes within your team to enhance its performance or stop its performance degrading.

How to use it

When the team is first established, it is relatively unproductive [A], and as members settle into their roles and responsibilities, understand their objectives and learn to work with each other, the productivity is relatively low [B]. As they begin to meet their objectives their performance rises [C]. If they are left together for too long in the same roles, their performance will start to level off [D] and ultimately degrade [E].

Before the curve reaches its peak, we need to introduce some change. The effect is to send the team through a second curve. Initially, the performance level will drop, but it will quickly pick up again. If we are to make changes at point C, we need to plan them before we get there, but we need to know when we have arrived at the planning stage [P], when we have reached point C and what changes to make – see Figure 73.4.

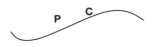

Figure 73.4 Sigmoid curve 4

At the early stages of team development we would typically sit with each member and set objectives. Somewhere along the rising curve of performance, team members begin to meet their objectives, but they still require a lot of intervention and direction from you, their manager. Like baby birds, they will return to mother for feeding. As they become more used to working together and develop greater understanding of how to fulfil their objectives, they begin to establish a routine, their performance improves, your level of intervention is vastly reduced and they become a well-oiled machine.

At this point, you need to use your intuition and take some risks. It is possible that the team could continue to work for some time at a high level of performance, but there is always the risk that they can become stale, the work becomes routine and they lack the spark that took them to this high performance level. Now it is time to make some changes. Here are some possibilities – their effectiveness will depend on the skills of the team, the level of autonomy you have in managing them and your skill and judgement as a manager:

1   Give them more stretching objectives to refocus them.

2   Rotate roles and responsibilities.

3   Take out the most talented member of the team and second them to another department. This works at several levels. It is good talent management because they learn new skills; it may be good succession planning if you can nurture skills that they can later bring back to your team; it gives a chance for aspiring 'stars' to take the star role vacated by your most talented team member. Now you may have one or two people vying for the role. Encourage them and give them every opportunity. After some weeks or months, bring back the original star and watch what happens – effectively you are reforming the team. Give the returning star and those who have taken that role coaching and mentoring roles so they can start to develop experience which will stand them in good stead should they move into a managerial role. It will give them experience of working at a new level and it will help to develop less experienced team members. It will reduce your management burden while helping to retain talented people before there is a possibility to promote them.

4   Bring in a new team member. The moment a new person joins, the whole team dynamic changes and after a settling-in period, the team's productivity should begin to rise again.

5   Give the team a new project, so all their roles and responsibilities change.

Final analysis

The sigmoid curve is a conceptual tool rather than a rigorous scientific one. There is a risk inherent in making changes too early when the team may have been able to work at a high level for some time before its performance levelled and degraded. There is a danger that too many changes induce change fatigue and team members become demotivated.

There is a danger, too, that you make the changes too late and the effort of bringing the team back to high performance is enormous. It is not a tool for the faint-hearted. It is, however, perhaps the only management tool that works on the basis of fixing things that are already working extremely well. A number of regular, small changes may be more effective than big changes and serve to keep driving up the team's performance while constantly engaging and motivating the team members.

Reference

Handy, C. (1995) *The Empty Raincoat: Making sense of the future.* London: Random House Business.

Tick-box and high-performance teams

74

The big picture

A tick-box culture is driven by rules, controls, systems and processes. A high-performance culture accepts that certain basic controls are needed as a platform from which to jump into high performance.

Imagine the scene: ABC Corporation employs 300 people. Every 1st March, the HR department sends a reminder to every manager in the corporation that they must set and agree objectives for their team members by 1st April. The managers dutifully sit down with their team members, agree some relatively SMART objectives and send a note to HR to say they have done it. On 1st October every year, HR sends a note to each manager reminding them to conduct appraisal interviews by 31st October. After a mad flurry of activity, considerable downtime in productivity and several further reminders from HR, the final appraisal is completed by around 15th November and managers and staff can relax again. A month later a new reminder appears, telling managers that they must have done their team members' personal development planning by the end of the calendar year. Duty done, and for a few quiet months ABC Corporation returns to normal. The objectives, appraisals and personal development plans are neatly filed, ready to be dusted off as the process starts again in March.

In XYZ Corporation, which also employs 300 people, managers rarely need a reminder to complete objective setting – it is done as a matter of course, because managers take a keen interest in the development of their staff. Objectives are truly SMART and designed to address development needs, stretch the team members and link through business plans to XYZ's business strategy.

Managers have agreed with their staff how they will jointly monitor progress against the objectives. They have looked again at the last personal development plan, removing any objective which they acknowledge has now been achieved, having an adult conversation about real development needs which are relevant to the individual, the team and the organisation. Before appraisal meetings, team members assess their own performance before meeting their managers to discuss progress and further areas for development. There is no blame, no finger pointing, and there are no surprises. A review of the past is relatively short, because managers have spoken regularly to each team member throughout the appraisal period.

ABC is the archetypal tick-box culture. People even talk about doing appraisals 'to shut HR up'. XYZ is the archetypal high-performance culture.

The examples here are based around HR systems and in reality could relate to any aspect of the business.

When to use it

Use the model as a regular reality check within your own team to ensure that your focus is on performance supported by systems, rather than systems driving your team's work.

How to use it

1 Review the major systems, processes, controls and procedures that are essential to the smooth running of your team's operations. When did you last examine them? Do they work? Do they create any additional burden for you or your staff? (Ask your staff!)

2 Do the systems, processes, controls and procedures support the performance of your team? Is there anything your team could do better, faster, more effectively, more efficiently if a control was reduced or removed?

3 Is there anything that is entirely driven by process? If you removed the process, would the team be able to operate equally well?

4 Are there any inherited systems which you continue to use without question?

5 Are you in any way driven by processes and controls?

6 Now, copy Figure 74.1 on to a piece of paper. The line represents a continuum between a tick-box culture and a high-performance culture. In reality, they are not polar opposites, but the diagram will serve as a jumping-off point for a review of your team's ethos.

Tick-box culture · High-performance culture

Figure 74.1 Tick-box culture vs. high-performance culture

7 Mark on the line where you see the team now in relation to the two cultures by writing the letter T on the line. Is the team's work more driven by process or by performance? Do you allow systems and processes to dictate how you work or to support your work?

8 If you consider that the culture of your team is moving more towards the tick-box end of the spectrum, draw an arrow pointing in that direction. If it is moving closer to a higher-performance culture, then draw an arrow pointing in that direction.

9 Now consider where the organisation might fit on this spectrum, mark an O on the line and an arrow to show its direction of travel.

10 Consider your own mindset. Where do you see yourself in relation to the two cultures? Write your initials on the line at the appropriate place and an arrow for your direction of travel.

11 Finally, consider where the team sees either you or itself (whichever you consider is more useful information) and mark that on the line with an arrow.

12 Review what you have drawn:

- Are all the marks in the same area?

    - If not, why not?

    - If so, is there a danger that you have become institutionalised and are not seeing the team's work as objectively as you could?

- Is the direction of travel the same for each marker?

    - If so, in which direction?

    - If not, why not? What are the constraints, whether self-imposed or imposed by the organisation? Are any of them imagined constraints?

- Why did you mark the line at these places?

    - Do you actually know or have you guessed?

    - What would you have to do to mark the diagram more accurately?

- What would have to happen to move any of the markers closer to where you believe they should be?

    - Are you in a position to make those changes?

    - Can you direct or influence others to make the changes?

- Do the position and direction of any of the markers frustrate you?

    - If you believe you are unable to change them, are you sufficiently resilient to live with that frustration?

This is just a small sample of the questions that this simple picture can generate. Share the model with your team, ask them to populate it and see whether your own picture matches theirs. If it does not, why is there a mismatch? Does that mismatch matter in terms of their performance, their expectations and their understanding of what you and the organisation expect of them?

Reasons for the mismatch could be specific to your organisation or your team's circumstances. More generically, they could be caused by poor communication, unspoken frustration at current systems and processes, or you as their manager shielding them from the (perceived) reality of the organisation.

Final analysis

Many of us talk about our organisation as though it is a distinct entity and separate from us. In reality, an organisation is a collective of people who, at least temporarily, choose to work under its flag. We *are* the organisation and when we complain about it, it is worth remembering that we are a part of it and that we do have the ability to make changes, to influence others to make changes and to introduce improvements.

As a manager you are judged by the quality of your team's work. If there are processes and systems that impede your team's performance, think about how you can begin to change them. Use some of the creative thinking tools in this book to assess where changes should be implemented (e.g. SCAMPER and brain-friendly brainstorming, each done with your team) and gradually start to introduce the changes you need to move your team further towards the high-performance culture.

As a manager you are a steward of your organisation and you leave a legacy. If you work with systems and processes that do not serve you, your team or the organisation well, and you do nothing to try to change them, this is both poor stewardship and a poor legacy to those who follow you into the organisation. The manager's role is not simply to maintain the status quo (a questionable state in changing times) but to improve the way that things are done. This little model will give you a head start in planning those improvements, enhancing your stewardship and creating a valuable legacy.

Reference

Hawkins, P. (ed.) (2014) *Leadership Team Coaching in Practice: Developing high-performing teams.* London and Philadelphia, PA: Kogan Page.

Extended Tuckman teamwork theory

75

The big picture

When a new team comes together, it will not immediately perform well. In 1965, psychologist Bruce Tuckman described four stages which every team goes through as it evolves – forming, storming, norming and performing. Around ten years later, Tuckman added an adjourning stage to the model. Others have suggested: dorming, mourning, transforming and reforming.

- **Forming**: members of the team are polite, wary, assessing each other. There is a lot of dependence on the leader for guidance. Processes are not yet established.

- **Storming**: team members start to vie for position. Conversation is less formal. Individuals may challenge each other and the leader. While they are more certain of the team's aims, power struggles and the formation of cliques may start to emerge.

- **Norming**: members are now clear about their roles and responsibilities and the team begins to feel more cohesive and united. Members show more respect to the leader who, in turn, is able to delegate more.

- **Performing**: the team now does what it was established to do. Performance rises as people settle into their roles. The leader has less need to intervene as members are able to work with less supervision and achieve their objectives.

- **Transforming/reforming**: the aim of this stage is to prevent the team reaching the *dorming* stage (below). Aware that, over time, performance may degrade, the team leader makes changes within the team, which may include setting new objectives, changing the team composition by taking people out or bringing new people in, job rotation, secondments and setting new or more stretching objectives. The idea is to *reform* the team and quickly send it back to the *forming* and *norming* stages.

- **Dorming** (also described as 'yawning'): the team has worked for some time like a well-oiled machine. Everyone knows what they have to do and the leader's role is more about monitoring and quality control than direct intervention. Over time, the work fails to stretch team members, who may settle into a rut, become complacent or bored. Performance begins to level off and ultimately degrade.

- **Adjourning**: the team is disbanded, either because it has served its purpose and achieved its goals or because it has become dysfunctional or irrelevant.

- **Mourning**: team members look back and reminisce about the 'good old days' when they worked together.

In reality, a team that stays together unchanged for too long becomes stagnant and performance degrades. The extended theory allows you to assess where your team is now (see Figure 75.1) and to take action to prevent or remedy that degradation in performance.

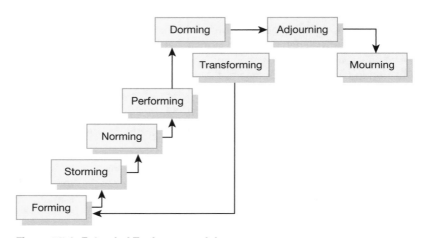

Figure 75.1 Extended Tuckman model

When to use it

Check progress against the model at least monthly in a non-project-based team and more regularly in a project-based environment.

How to use it

Use the model to check the stage your team has reached so that you can plan the transformations needed to ensure that you are getting the best possible performance from everyone. The ideal time to make a change is when the level of performance is still rising, rather than waiting until it has begun to level and decline.

See the sigmoid curve (Chapter 73) for details of the types of change you can make to maintain high performance.

Final analysis

Tuckman's original model seems to suggest that a team that works together over time will maintain high levels of performance. In reality, time breeds a levelling and degradation of performance, so the added levels are a better reflection of reality. Rather than treat the model as an abstract concept, use it as a working tool, ensuring that you know exactly where your team is at any time in its evolution. Use it in conjunction with the sigmoid curve (see Chapter 73) as a planning tool.

Reference

Tuckman, B. (1965) 'Developmental sequence in small groups', *Psychological Bulletin,* 63(6): 384–389.

What did you think of this book?

We're really keen to hear from you about this book, so that we can make our publishing even better.

Please log on to the following website and leave us your feedback.

It will only take a few minutes and your thoughts are invaluable to us.

www.pearsoned.co.uk/bookfeedback

Index

abstract conceptualisation 96–7
accelerated learning
  big picture 90
  final analysis 91–2
  how to use 90–1
  when to use 90
accommodating conflict mode 151–2
accommodator learning style 97–9
achievable goals 121–2, 176, 181–2
act component of decision making
    model 44–5
action
  and affirm, in solution-focused coaching 123–4
  in emotional intelligence 61
  and inaction 31, 173
  as 'living fully' 242
  rising and falling, in stories 137
  setting behavioural objectives 184–5
  stage in ladder of inference 41–3
  stage of coaching model 118–19
action-centred leadership
  big picture 207
  final analysis 209
  how to use 207–9
  when to use 207
active experimentation 96–7
active listening
  big picture 102, 118
  final analysis 103
  how to use 103
  resources 104
  when to use 102
activist learning style 98
Adair, John 207, 209
adapt stage of SCAMPER tool 167
adaptive child state 246
adjourning stage of teamwork model 259, 260
adult ego state 245–8
adversarial model of negotiation 221–2
aesthetic needs 17
affiliative leadership style 216, 217
affirm and action stage of solution-focused
    coaching 123–4
affirmations see positive affirmations
aggressive approach to work 111
aggressive people 70
agreement
  best alternative to negotiated 224–5
  stage of negotiation 229, 230
  wise 226
agreements (relationships)
  always do your best 242

being impeccable with your word 240
  big picture 239–40
  don't make assumptions 241–2
  don't take anything personally 241
  final analysis 242
  how to use 240–2
  when to use 240
Allen, David 83–4
analysis
  part of brain 93, 191
  stage of negotiation 229, 230
anchoring calm state
  big picture 71
  final analysis 72
  how to use 71–2
  when to use 71
Argyris, Chris 41
ask, as step of law of attraction 29
assertiveness 111
  broken record 112–13
  in conflict model 151–3
  fogging 114–15
assimilator learning style 97–9
associative language 203
assumptions
  challenging 159–60
  making 241–2
  stage in ladder of inference 41–2
attention, listening with 107, 227
attribution theory 197–9
auditory people 144–5, 146
autocratic leadership style 49–51
automatic pilot 61–2
automatic thoughts 25, 26
autonomy 21–2
avoiding conflict mode 151–2

bargaining see distributive bargaining; integrative
    bargaining
BATNA (best alternative to negotiated agreement)
    224–5
bee metaphor 138–40
behaviour, drivers of 18–20
behavioural objectives 184–5
beliefs 4, 26, 41–3
believe, as step of law of attraction 29
Benziger, Katherine 93
Benziger's thinking styles assessment
  big picture 93–4
  final analysis 95
  how to use 94–5
  when to use 94

Berg, Insoo Kim 123
Berne, Eric 245–7
bestial intelligence 67
Betari box
  big picture 149
  final analysis 150
  how to use 150
  when to use 150
bilateral brain theory
  big picture 191–2
  final analysis 193
  how to use 192–3
  when to use 192
blockers 35–7
bodily–kinaesthetic intelligence 67
body language 103, 107, 113, 134–5, 243–4
Boyd, John 44–5
brain
  basal left quadrant 93–4
  basal right quadrant 94
  bilateral, theory 191–3
  frontal left quadrant 93
  frontal right quadrant 94
  impact of storytelling 136
  left side of 191
  right side of 191–2
brain-friendly brainstorming
  big picture 156
  final analysis 157–8
  how to use 156–7
  when to use 156
brainstorming 36, 138–40, 156–8, 161, 166
broken record technique
  big picture 112
  final analysis 113
  how to use 113
  when to use 112
Byrne, Rhonda 28

calm state, anchoring 71–2
CASE – behavioural objectives
  big picture 184
  final analysis 185
  how to use 184–5
  when to use 184
causal dimensions (attribution theory) 197–8
challenge
  as characteristic of stress-hardy people 54–5
  as goal-setting principle 178
challenging assumptions
  big picture 159
  final analysis 160
  how to use 159–60
  when to use 159
change see personal change
child ego state 245–8
choice
  to be exercised regularly 24
  making best possible 38
  theory 18–20

clarity, as goal-setting principle 177
CLEAR model
  big picture 118
  final analysis 119
  how to use 118–19
  when to use 118
close stage of negotiation 229, 230
coaching 117
  CLEAR model 118–19
  GROW model 120–2
  solution-focused 123–5
coaching leadership style 206, 218
cognitive needs 17
cognitive restructuring
  big picture 25
  final analysis 26
  how to use 25–6
  when to use 25
collaborating conflict mode 151–3
collaborative leadership style 49, 51, 217
collaborative problem solving 220
collect, as step in GTD 83–4
collectivist society 17
combine stage of SCAMPER tool 167
commands, embedded 194–6
commitment
  as characteristic of stress-hardy people 54–5
  as goal-setting principle 178
communication 127
  DISC model 128–33
  influential 192–3
  matching and mirroring 134–5
  storytelling 136–42
  VAK tool 143–6
  see also Johari window
competencies 58–9, 250
competing conflict mode 151–2
complementary interactions 246
compliance 128–9, 130, 132
compliments 7
compromising conflict mode 151, 153
concentration 79, 103
concrete experience 96–7
conflict management 148
  Betari box 149–50
  Thomas–Kilmann conflict mode instrument 151–3
  through stories 141
conflict mode instrument 151–3
consultative leadership style 49–51
content reframing 6
context, for setting behavioural objectives 184–5
continuous improvement 31
contract stage of coaching 118, 119
control
  as characteristic of stress-hardy people 54–5
  as level of influence 202–4
  locus of 197–9
controllability (attribution theory) 197–9
converger learning style 97–9

cooperativeness 151–3
Coué, Émile 4
covert leadership
    big picture 210–11
    final analysis 212
    how to use 211–12
    when to use 211
Covey, Stephen R. 30–1, 80, 242
Covey's time matrix
    big picture 80
    final analysis 82
    how to use 81–2
    when to use 81
creativity 155
    brain-friendly brainstorming 156–8
    challenging assumptions 159–60
    PMI tool 161–2
    random word technique 163–5
    SCAMPER tool 166–7
critical listening
    big picture 105
    final analysis 106
    how to use 105–6
    when to use 105
crossed interactions 247–8

de Shazer, Steve 123
debate stage of negotiation 229, 230
decision making see problem solving and decision
    making
decision model 49–51
Deming, Edward 45
directive leadership style 216
DISC model
    big picture 128–30
    final analysis 133
    how to use 131–2
    when to use 130
disclosure through stories 138
dissociative language 203
distributive bargaining
    big picture 221
    final analysis 222
    how to use 222
    when to use 221–2
diverger learning style 97–9
doing
    learning stage/style expressed as 97, 99
    less focus on, for meditation 74
    as step in GTD 83, 84
dominance, as element of DISC model 128–9,
    131–2
dorming stage of teamwork 259–60
drivers of human behaviour
    according to Glasser 18–20
    according to Pink 21

Eberle, Robert 166, 167
education through stories 138
EEC model 169

big picture 170
final analysis 171
how to use 170–1
when to use 170
EENC model 169
    big picture 172
    final analysis 174
    how to use 172–4
    when to use 172
ego states 245–8
Eisenhower, Dwight D. 80
eliminate stage of SCAMPER tool 167
Ellis, Albert 25
embedded commands
    big picture 194
    final analysis 196
    how to use 194–5
    when to use 194
emotional intelligence
    big picture 60
    final analysis 62
    how to use 60–2
    self-awareness as cornerstone of 57
    when to use 60
empathy
    as component of relationship listening
        107–8
    for working with others 30, 61
engagement through stories 138
evaluation, for setting behavioural
        objectives 184–5
existential intelligence 67
explore hidden attitudes 224–5
explore stage of coaching 119
extended Tuckman teamwork theory
    big picture 259–60
    final analysis 261
    how to use 260–1
    when to use 260
external power 189
extroverted temperament 128–9, 131

4Ps of persuasion
    big picture 188
    final analysis 189–90
    how to use 188–9
    when to use 188
feedback
    360° 58–9
    as goal-setting principle 177–8
    see also Johari window
feedback, giving 169
    EEC model 170–1
    EENC model 172–4
feeling
    learning stage/style expressed as 96–7, 99
    people 145–6
    quadrant of brain 94
fish frying analogy 210–11
Fisher, Roger 226

focus 79
   for active listening 103
   areas of, for leadership 208–9
   on imperatives, through stories 141
   on interests, not positions 226–7
   soft 73–4, 76
   see also reticular activating system (RAS)
fogging technique
   big picture 114
   final analysis 115
   how to use 114–15
   when to use 114
force field analysis
   big picture 35
   final analysis 37
   how to use 35–7
   when to use 35
forming stage of teamwork 259–60
free child state 246
freedom
   as driver of human behaviour 18
   motivational ideas for 20
   needs of people driven by 19
Freytag, Gustav 136–7
fun and enjoyment
   as driver of human behaviour 18
   motivational ideas for 20
   needs of people driven by 19

Gardner, Howard 66, 67
getting things done (GTD)
   big picture 83
   final analysis 84
   how to use 83–4
   when to use 83
Glasser, William 15, 17–18, 20
Glasser's choice theory
   big picture 18
   final analysis 20
   how to use 19–20
   when to use 19
goal setting 176
   CASE – behavioural objectives 184–5
   Locke and Latham's principles 177–8
   reticular activating system 179–80
   SMART goals 181–3
goal stage of GROW model 120–1
Goleman, Daniel 57, 60–1, 213
GROW model
   big picture 120
   final analysis 122
   how to use 121–2
   when to use 120
GTD see getting things done (GTD)

Haanel, Charles 28
happiness
   effect on productivity 3
   as inalienable right 3
   positive affirmations 4–5
   positive mental attitude and content reframing 6–7

hardiness
   big picture 54
   final analysis 55
   how to use 55
   when to use 54
Harvard principled negotiation
   big picture 226
   final analysis 228
   how to use 226–7
   when to use 226
Hawkins, Peter 118
hearing people 144–5, 146
helpers 35–7
Herzberg, Frederick 15, 22, 207
hierarchy of needs 16–17
high-performance teams see tick-box
      and high-performance teams
Hill, Napoleon 28
Honey, Peter 96, 98
hygiene factors 15, 22

ideal solutions in negotiation 223–5
imperatives, focus on, through stories 141
inaction/action 31, 173
independence (of self-mastery) 30
individual focus 208–9
individualistic society 17
influence 187
   bilateral brain theory 191–3
   as element of DISC model 128–30, 132
   embedded commands 194–6
   as level of influence 202–3
   locus of control 197–9
   spheres of 202–4
   through stories 140–1
   see also persuasion
Ingham, Harry 63
integrative bargaining
   big picture 223
   final analysis 225
   how to use 223–5
   when to use 223
interdependence (working with others) 30
interest/impact stage of presentation 235–6
internal power 188–9
International Day of Happiness 3
interpersonal intelligence 67–8
intrapersonal intelligence 67–8
INTRO for presentation
   big picture 234
   final analysis 236
   how to use 235–6
   when to use 234
introverted temperament 128–9, 131
intuition quadrant of brain 94
irrational thoughts 25–6
is/is not problem solving technique
   big picture 38
   final analysis 40
   how to use 39–40
   when to use 38

Jackson, Paul Z. 123
Jago, Arthur 49
Johari window
    big picture 63–4
    final analysis 65
    how to use 64–5
    when to use 64
Johnson, Barry 46–8
Jung, Carl 95, 128

Kabat-Zinn, Jon 75
Kepner, Charles 38
Kilmann, Ralph 151, 153
kinaesthetic
    intelligence 67
    people 145–6
know-how stage of solution-focused coaching
    model 123–4
Kobasa, Suzanne 54
Kolb, David 96–9
Kolb, Honey and Mumford learning styles
    big picture 96–8
    final analysis 99
    how to use 98–9
    when to use 98

ladder of inference
    big picture 41–2
    final analysis 43
    how to use 43
    when to use 42
Lao Tzu 210
Latham, Gary 177
law of attraction 6, 180
    big picture 28
    final analysis 29
    how to use 28–9
    when to use 28
law of primacy and recency 234
law of requisite variety 218
leadership 206
    action-centred 207–9
    covert 210–12
    types 49–51
leadership styles
    big picture 213
    final analysis 218
    how to use 213–16
    understanding 216–18
    when to use 213
learning 89
    accelerated 90–2
    Benziger's thinking styles assessment 93–5
    Kolb, Honey and Mumford learning styles 96–9
Lewin, Kurt 35
linguistic intelligence 66, 68
listen stage of coaching 118
listening skills 101
    active listening 102–4
    critical listening 105–6
    relationship listening 107–8

little professor child state 246
Loci method
    big picture 10
    final analysis 11
    how to use 10–11
    when to use 10
Locke and Latham's principles
    big picture 177
    final analysis 178
    how to use 177–8
    when to use 177
Locke, Edwin 177
locus of control
    big picture 197–8
    final analysis 199
    how to use 198
    when to use 198
logical–mathematical intelligence 67
love and belonging
    as driver of human behaviour 18
    motivational ideas for 19
    needs of people driven by 19
Luft, Joseph 63

Maltz, Maxwell 61
Marston, William Moulton 128
Maslow, Abraham 15–17, 18, 207
Maslow's hierarchy of needs
    big picture 16
    final analysis 17
    how to use 17
    when to use 17
mastery
    as driver of human behaviour 21
    self 30
matching and mirroring
    big picture 134
    final analysis 135
    how to use 134–5
    when to use 134
McKergow, Mark 123
measurable goals 181–2
meditation
    big picture 73
    final analysis 74
    how to use 73–4
    when to use 73
memory and recall 9
    Loci method 10–11
    number/rhyme method 12–13
memory palace see Loci method
mental attitude see positive mental attitude
metaphor, use of 91, 138–40, 141–2
micro-management 211, 212
mindfulness
    big picture 75
    final analysis 76
    how to use 76
    resources 77
    when to use 75
mirroring 134–5, 243–4

mitote 239, 241
modify stage of SCAMPER tool 167
moral intelligence 67
motivation 15
   Glasser's choice theory 18–20
   Maslow's hierarchy of needs 16–17
   Pink's model 21–2
mourning stage of teamwork 259, 260
multiple intelligences
   big picture 66–7
   final analysis 68
   how to use 67–8
   when to use 67
Mumford, Alan 96, 98
musical cadence 145, 194–5
musical intelligence 66
Myers–Briggs Type Indicator 95

naguals 239
natural child state 246
naturalist intelligence 67
needs
   in EENC model 172–3
   hierarchy of 16–17
   stage of presentation 234–5
negative language 200–1
negative reactions 7, 149–50
negative thoughts 26, 28, 75
negotiation 220
   distributive bargaining 221–2
   Harvard principled 226–8
   integrative bargaining 223–5
   RADPAC 229–31
New Age 7, 180, 242
Niebuhr, Reinhold 204
norming stage of teamwork 259–60
nothing at all, as level of influence 202–4
number/rhyme method
   big picture 12
   final analysis 13
   how to use 12–13
   when to use 12

objective criteria, insisting on, as negotiation
      principle 226, 227
objective setting *see* SMART goals
objectives
   behavioural 184–5
   stage of presentation 234, 235–6
OODA (observe, orient, decide, act) loop
   big picture 44
   final analysis 45
   how to use 44–5
   when to use 44
options
   inventing, for mutual gain 226–7
   stage of GROW model 120, 122
orchestral conductor analogy 211
organise, as step in GTD 83, 84
OSKAR coaching model 123–5

Oswald, Andrew 3
outcome stage of OSKAR model 123

pacesetting leadership style 216, 217–18
parent ego state 245–8
participative leadership style 216, 217
passive approach to work 111
Pavlov, Ivan 71
people focused temperament 128–9, 131
performance
   culture of high 255–8
   for persuasion 188, 189
   sigmoid curve for high 251–4
performing stage of teamwork 259–60
personal change 24
   cognitive restructuring 25–7
   laws of attraction/*The Secret* 28–9
   seven habits 30–2
persuasion 187
   4Ps of 188–90
   positive language 200–1
   see also influence
Pink, Daniel H. 21–2
Pink's model of motivation
   big picture 21
   final analysis 22
   how to use 21–2
   when to use 21
plot development model 137
PMI (plus, minus, interesting) tool
   big picture 161
   final analysis 162
   how to use 161
   when to use 161
polarity management
   big picture 46
   final analysis 48
   how to use 47–8
   when to use 47
politeness, for persuasion 188, 189
positioning, for persuasion 188, 189
positive affirmations
   big picture 4
   final analysis 5
   how to use 5
   when to use 4
positive language
   big picture 200
   final analysis 201
   how to use 200–1
   when to use 200
positive mental attitude
   big picture 6
   final analysis 7
   how to use 7
   when to use 6
power and status
   as driver of human behaviour 18
   motivational ideas for 19
   needs of people driven by 19

power, for persuasion 188–9
pragmatist learning style 98
presentation 233–6
proactivity 30
problem solving and decision making 34
  force field analysis 35–7
  is/is not technique 38–40
  ladder of inference 41–3
  OODA loop 44–5
  polarity management 46–8
  Vroom–Yetton–Jago decision model 49–51
process, as step in GTD 83, 84
proposal stage of negotiation 229, 230
purpose, as driver of human behaviour 21–2
put to another use stage of SCAMPER tool 167
pyramid designs 16, 137

race metaphor 141–2
RADPAC
  big picture 229
  final analysis 231
  how to use 229–30
  when to use 229
random word technique
  big picture 163
  final analysis 165
  how to use 163–4
  when to use 163
range stage of presentation 234, 235–6
rapport building
  big picture 243
  final analysis 244
  how to use 243–4
  mirroring for 134–5, 243–4
  stage of negotiation 229–30
  when to use 243
realistic solutions in negotiation 223–5
reality stage of GROW model 120–2
recall see memory and recall
receive, as step of law of attraction 29
reflective observation 96–7
reflector learning style 98
reforming stage of teamwork 259, 260
reframing see content reframing
relationship listening
  big picture 107
  final analysis 108
  how to use 107–8
  when to use 107
relationships 238
  four agreements 239–42
  and rapport building 229–30, 243–4
  relationship listening 107–8
  relationship management 61
  transactional analysis 245–8
relevant goals 181, 182–3
resilience 53–5
reticular activating system (RAS)
  big picture 179
  final analysis 180

  how to use 180
  when to use 180
reverse/rearrange stage of SCAMPER tool 167
review
  stage of coaching models 119, 124
  as step in GTD 83, 84
rhyme/number method 12–13
Rose, Colin 90
Ruiz, Don Miguel 239–42

7 Habits of Highly Effective People 30–2, 80, 242
scale stage of OSKAR model 124
SCAMPER tool
  big picture 166
  final analysis 167
  how to use 167
  when to use 166
The Secret 28–9
self-actualisation 16, 17
self-awareness 57
  360° feedback 58–9
  emotional intelligence 60–2
  Johari window 63–5
  multiple intelligences 66–8
self-confidence 70
self-mastery 30
self-regulation 61
selling through stories 140
Senge, Peter 41
senses tool
  for communication 143–6
  for learning 90–2
sensing quadrant of brain 93–4
separating people from problem, as negotiation
    principle 226–7
Serenity Prayer 204
seven habits
  big picture 30–1
  final analysis 31–2
  how to use 31
  when to use 31
sigmoid curve
  big picture 251–2
  final analysis 253–4
  how to use 252–3
  when to use 252
simile, use of 91
SMART goals 178, 184, 255
  big picture 181
  final analysis 183
  how to use 182–3
  when to use 182
social awareness 61
solution-focused coaching
  big picture 123
  final analysis 124
  how to use 123–4
  resources 124–5
  when to use 123
spatial intelligence 67

specific goals 181, 182
spheres of influence
    big picture 202–3
    final analysis 204
    how to use 203–4
    when to use 203
spiritual intelligence 67
stability (attribution theory) 197, 198
standards, for setting behavioural objectives 184–5
status *see* power and status
steadiness, as element of DISC model 128–9,
    130, 132
storming stage of teamwork 259, 260
storytelling
    big picture 136–7
    final analysis 142
    how to use 137–42
    when to use 137
strategy, outlining, through stories 141–2
stress-hardy people *see* hardiness
stress management 70
    anchoring calm state 71–2
    meditation 73–4
    mindfulness 75–7
submissive approach to work 111
substitute stage of SCAMPER tool 167
support, as component of relationship listening 107
survival
    as driver of human behaviour 18
    as physiological need 19
    senses 143
synergising 31

360° feedback
    big picture 58
    final analysis 59
    how to use 58–9
    when to use 58
Tao Te Ching 210–11
task complexity, as goal-setting principle 178
task focused
    leadership 208–9
    temperament 128–9, 131
team focused leadership 208–9
teamwork 250
    extended Tuckman theory 259–61
    Sigmoid curve 251–4
    tick-box and high-performance teams 255–8
theorist learning style 98
thinking
    learning stage/style expressed as 97, 99
    quadrant of brain 93
    styles assessment 93–5
Thomas, Ken 151
Thomas–Kilmann conflict mode instrument
    big picture 151–2
    final analysis 153
    how to use 152–3
    when to use 152

tick-box and high-performance teams
    big picture 255–6
    final analysis 258
    how to use 256–8
    when to use 256
time management 79
    Covey's time matrix 80–2
    getting things done (GTD) 83–4
timebound goals 181, 183
timing stage of presentation 235–6
Toltecs 239
transactional analysis (TA)
    big picture 245–7
    final analysis 248
    how to use 247–8
    when to use 247
transcendence needs 17
transforming stage of teamwork 259, 260
Tregoe, Benjamin 38
Tuckman, Bruce 259

ulterior interactions 247
Ury, William 226
US Declaration of Independence 3

VAK (visual, auditory, kinaesthetic) tool
    big picture 143
    final analysis 146
    how to use 144–6
    when to use 143
vision, outlining, through stories 141–2
visionary leadership style 216
visual people 144, 146
visualisation 13, 28, 72
Vroom, Victor 22, 49
Vroom–Yetton–Jago decision model
    big picture 49
    final analysis 51
    how to use 50–1
    when to use 50

watching, learning stage/style expressed as 97, 99
way forward stage of GROW model 120, 122
Weiner, Bernard 197
Weiner's attribution theory 197–9
wheel of life
    big picture 85
    final analysis 87
    how to use 85–6
    when to use 85
win–lose negotiation 220, 221–2
win–win thought 30
wise agreement 226
work–life balance 79, 85–7
working with others 30–1

Yetton, Philip 49

zero–sum negotiation 221–2

Do you want your people to be the very best at what they do?

Talk to us about how we can help.

As the world's leading learning company, we know a lot about what your people need in order to be better at what they do.

Whatever subject or skills you've got in mind (from presenting or persuasion to coaching or communication skills), and at whatever level (from new-starters through to top executives) we can help you deliver tried-and-tested, essential learning straight to your workforce – whatever they need, whenever they need it and wherever they are.

Talk to us today about how we can:

- Complement and support your existing learning and development programmes
- Enhance and augment your people's learning experience
- Match your needs to the best of our content
- Customise, brand and change it to make a better fit
- Deliver cost-effective, great value learning content that's proven to work.

Contact us today:
corporate.enquiries@pearson.com